SWING TRADING

A Beginner's Guide To Trade For Profits With The Best Trading Strategies, Using Money Management, Market Psychology, Technical Analysis And Trading Tools

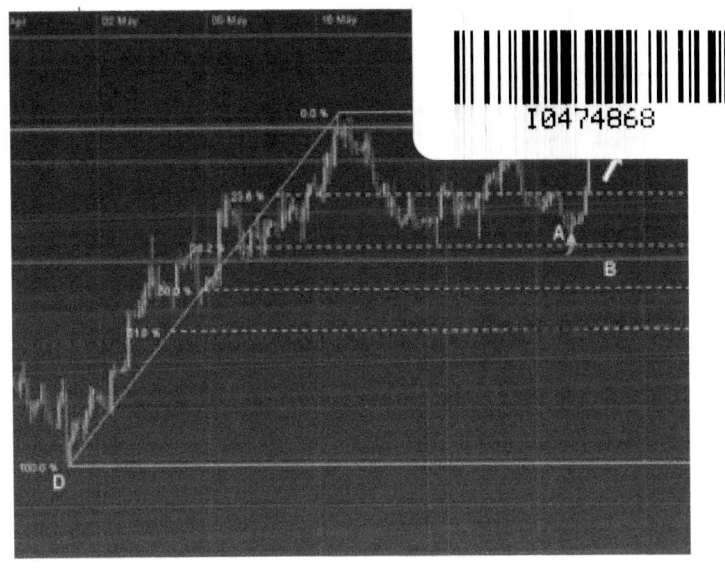

A Book By:

RICHARD JONES

i

CONTENTS

INTRODUCTION

Swing trading consolidates significant and specialized examination to get earth shattering value developments while staying away from inactive occasions. The advantages of this kind of trading are an increasingly effective utilization of capital and higher returns, and the disadvantages are higher commissions and greater instability.

Swing trading can be difficult for the standard retail trader. The expert traders have more understanding, influence, data, and lower commissions; notwithstanding, they are constrained by the instruments they are permitted to trade, the hazard they are equipped for taking on and their huge measure of capital. (Enormous establishments trade in sizes too huge to move all through stocks rapidly.) Knowledgeable retail traders can exploit these things to benefit reliably in the commercial center. Here is the idea that a decent everyday swing trading routine and system may look like....and you how you can be comparatively fruitful in your trading exercises.

Pre-Market

The retail swing trader will frequently start his day at 6 am EST, a long time before the opening chime. The time before the opening is significant for getting a general feel for the day's market, discovering potential trades, making a day by day watch list and, at long last, determining the status of existing positions.

Market Overview

The primary assignment of the day is to make up for lost time with the most recent news and advancements in the business sectors. The speediest method to do this is using the digital TV slot CNBC or trustworthy sites, for example, Market Watch. The trader needs to watch out for three things precisely:

In general, market notion (bullish/bearish, critical financial reports, expansion, cash, abroad trading sessions, and so on.)

Discover Potential Trades

Next, the trader will examine for potential trades for the afternoon. Regularly, swing traders will enter a situation with a central impetus and oversee or leave the situation with the guide of specialized investigation. There are two great approaches to discover major impetuses:

Extraordinary chances: These are best found using SEC filings and, now and again, feature news. Such open doors may incorporate starting open contributions (IPOs), insolvencies, insider purchasing, buyouts, takeovers, mergers, restructurings, acquisitions, and other comparative occasions. Ordinarily, these are found by checking certain SEC filings, for example, S-4 and 13D. This can be effectively finished with the assistance of destinations, for instance, SECFilings.com, which will send notifications when such a documenting is made. These sorts of chances frequently convey a lot of hazards. However, they convey numerous prizes to the individuals who cautiously look into every opportunity. These sortsof plays include the swing trader purchasing when most are selling and selling when every other person is buying, trying to "blur" eruptions to news and occasions.

The segment plays: These are best found by investigating the news or counseling decent money related data sites to discover which areas are performing great. For instance, you can tell that the vitality area is hot essentially by checking a prominent vitality trade traded support (like IYE) or examining the news for notices of the vitality segment. Traders searching for higher hazard and higher returns may search out increasingly darken divisions, for example, coal or titanium. These are regularly a lot harder to break down, yet they can yield a lot of more prominent returns. These sorts of plays include the swing trader becoming tied up with patterns at fortunate occasions and riding the patterns until there are indications of inversion or retracement.

Graph breaks are a third kind of chance accessible to swing traders. They usually are intensely traded stocks that are close to a key help or obstruction level. Swing traders will search for a few different kinds of examples intended to anticipate breakouts or breakdowns, for example, triangles, channels, Wolfe Waves, Fibonacci levels, Gann levels, and others. Note that outline breaks are just significant if there is adequate enthusiasm for the stock. These kinds of plays include the swing trader purchasing after a breakout and selling again presently at the following obstruction level.

Make a Watch List

The following stage is to make a watch rundown of stocks for the afternoon. These are essentially stocks that have a primary impetus and a shot at being a decent trade. Some swing traders like to keep a dry-delete board alongside their trading stations with an arranged rundown of chances, section costs, target costs, and stop-misfortune costs.

Check Existing Positions

At last, in the pre-advertise hours, the trader must determine the status of their current positions, investigating the news to ensure that nothing material has happened to the stock medium-term. This should be possible by primarily composing the stock image into a new administration, for example, Google News. Next, traders verify whether any filings have been made via looking through the SEC's EDGAR database. If there is material data, it ought to be broken down to decide if it influences the present trading plan. A trader may likewise need to modify their stop-misfortune, and take-benefit focuses accordingly.

Market Hours

The market hours are a period of watching and trading. Many swing traders take a gander at level II cites, which will demonstrate who is purchasing and selling and what sums they are trading. Those originating from the universe of day trading will likewise frequently check which market creator is making the trades (this can sign traders into who is behind the market producer's trades), and furthermore know about head-counterfeit offers and asks set to confound retail traders.

When a suitable trade has been found and entered, traders start to search for an exit. This is regularly done utilizing specialized investigation. Many swing traders like to use Fibonacci augmentations, straightforward obstruction levels, or cost by volume. In a perfect world, this is done before the trade has even been put, yet a great deal will regularly rely upon the day's trading. Also, alterations may be made later, contingent upon future trading. When in doubt, be that as it may, you ought to never change a situation to go out on a limb (e.g., move a stop-misfortune down): possibly modify benefit taking dimensions if trading keeps on looking bullish, or alter stop-misfortune levels upward to secure benefits.

Entering trades is frequently a more significant amount of a craftsmanship than a science, and it will, in general, rely upon the day's trading movement. Trade the executives and leaving, then again, ought to dependably be an exact science.

Nightfall Market

Nightfall trading is infrequently utilized as an opportunity to place trades because the market is illiquid, and the spread is frequently an excessive amount to justify. The most significant segment of twilight trading is execution assessment. It is essential to painstakingly record all trades and thoughts for both assessment purposes and execution assessment. Execution assessment includes investigating all trading action and identifying things that need improvement. At long last, a trader should audit their open positions one final time, giving specific consideration to night-time profit declarations, or other material occasions that may affect possessions.

Taking a gander at the day by day schedule of the common swing trader, it is obvious that the pre-showcase routine is principal to effective trading. This is when trading openings are found and the day is arranged. Market hours are essentially a period of entering and leaving positions, not conceiving any new plans. Lastly, night-time is only an opportunity to audit the trades for the afternoon and survey execution. Embracing an everyday trading routine, for example, this one can enable you to improve trading and at last beat market returns. It just takes some significant assets and appropriate arranging and planning.

SWING TRADING BASICS: WHAT IT IS AND HOW IT WORKS

Swing Trading is a momentary stock trading style. You take little benefits, cut misfortunes snappier, and hold stocks for less time. To make it work, your principles for trading should be specific to the shorter period. In spite of the fact that the additions may be littler, the shorter holding time frame implies you can intensify your increases into huge benefits after some time. Here are the essentials of executing a swing trading system.

Swing Trading Strategy: Smaller Gains, Smaller Losses

As opposed to focusing on a 20% to 25% benefit for a large portion of your trades, a progressively humble 5% to 10% will be the primary benefit objective. The difference is to a great extent because of the holding time frame. Swing trades didn't take place months ago. It's increasingly similar to two or three weeks. By taking the little additions, frequently in transit up, you get most of a speedy move and evade the territories when the stock solidifies. Try not to anticipate selling at the top constantly. You'll regularly observe stocks go up more and kick yourself for selling too soon. Be that as it may, you'll additionally, in general, keep away from market amendments.

When you take benefits in transit up, if no new arrangements present themselves to supplant the sold stocks, you've normally diminished your introduction. Swing trading system put IBD's Swing Trader in real money right on time in the 2018 Q4 remedy and did likewise for the financial exchange revision in February and March of a year ago. You may finish up getting out too soon yet you can generally repurchase stocks if they recoup.

While you are taking benefits rapidly for most stocks, at times, you may have enough starting solidarity to warrant giving a stock more space to run. Because of an incredible hole up, Swing Trader neared its 10% benefit objective for Fibria Celulose (FBR) in only two or three days. We sold half and let the rest of for an increase of 20% in only 15 days.

Obviously, only one out of every odd stock thought will work. Slicing misfortunes rapidly is critical to keeping your portfolio sound. You can have just a large portion of your trades end positive and still make a great deal of cash as long as you keep your misfortunes little contrasted with your additions.

Swing Trading Example: Paylocity Stock

Specialized examination assumes a bigger job in a swing trading methodology, yet it's still a great practice to concentrate on organizations with excellent essentials. Take the Paylocity (PCTY) stock. It was under thought for Swing Trader with the ideal Composite Rating of 99. Yet, there must be some sort of revision that offers you the open door for purchase. In the case of purchasing a breakout through an opposition or an inversion, a redress goes before the buy.

On May 9, Paylocity stock destroyed back to a purchase point around 91.70 and discovered help (1). The market activity on Swing Trader effectively turned wary the day preceding, going to sideways, as did the market standpoint in The Big Picture in its change to upswing under strain. The securities exchange declined on May 13 as the Nasdaq composite and S&P 500 cut through their 50-day moving normal lines. We exchanged Swing Trader market activity to a downtrend, and The Big Picture called the market in remedy. Strangely, Paylocity stock held over its past low on May 9, indicating relative quality (2).

That is the sort of specialized activity we search for notwithstanding the crucial quality. At only two or three weeks, it was unreasonably short for any of our customary base examples. In any case, for a swing trading methodology, the shorter holding time frame considers shorter unions.

On May 16, the Nasdaq composite and S&P 500 got back over their 50-day moving normal lines. Our swing trading methodology was as yet careful of potential securities exchange headwinds. In any case, if the market bounces back proceeded, it could be useful for at any rate a transient swing trade. That day, the overwhelming trading volume went with a solid move in Paylocity stock as it cleared the 100 imprints (3). As the revision in Paylocity was gentle up until now, contrasted with the securities exchange, the relative quality line was at that point in the new high ground (3). By the nearby, we previously had a 3% benefit from our entrance on Swing Trader.

Sadly, the benefits didn't last. Market lists fell appropriate back beneath the 50-day moving normal line the following day, and we evacuated Paylocity stock right on time to secure benefit (4). Taking increases rapidly in an intense market is a colossal advantage of swing trading procedure. The market declined, and we evaded the trade turning negative on us and rather left with a 1.4% increase. That may not be a great figure but rather think about what it benefited from a solitary day in an extreme market.

Duplicate that regularly enough, and you'll have an incredible year as your increases compound.

How Swing Trades Works

Swing trading tries to exploit the upward and descending "swings" in the cost of security. Traders plan to catch little moves inside a bigger in general pattern. Swing traders expect to make a lot of little successes that mean significant returns. For instance, different traders may hold up five months to win a 25% benefit, while swing traders may acquire 5% increases week by week and surpass the other trader's additions over the long haul.

Most swing traders utilize day by day graphs (like an hour, 24 hours, 48 hours, and so on.) to pick the best passage or leave point. Be that as it may, some may utilize shorter time allotment graphs, for example, 4-hour or hourly outlines.

Swing Trades versus Day Trading

Swing trading and day trading seem comparable in certain regards. The fundamental factor separating the two procedures is the holding position time. While swing traders may hold stocks medium-term to a little while, day trades close inside minutes or before the end of the market.

Informal investors don't hold their positions medium-term. This regularly implies they abstain from exposing their situations to dangers coming about because of news declarations. Their increasingly continuous trading results in higher exchange costs, which can considerably diminish their benefits. They frequently trade with an influence so as to expand benefits from little value changes.

Swing traders are exposed to the unusualness of medium-term chances that may result in significant value developments. Swing traders can check their positions occasionally and make a move when basic focuses are come to. Not at all like day trading, swing trading does not require consistent checking, since the trades keep going for a few days or weeks.

Trading Strategies

Swing traders can utilize the accompanying systems to search for noteworthy trading openings:

#1 Fibonacci retracement

Traders can utilize a Fibonacci retracement marker to identify backing and obstruction levels. Given this pointer, they can discover showcase inversion openings. The Fibonacci retracement levels of 61.8%, 38.2%, and 23.6% are accepted to uncover conceivable inversion levels. A trader may enter a purchase trade when the cost is in a descending pattern and appears to discover support at the 61.8% retracement level from its past high.

#2 T-line trading

Traders utilize the T-line on a diagram to settle on a choice on the best time to enter or leave a trade. When security closes over the T-line, it means that the cost will keep on rising. When the security closes beneath the T-line, it means that the cost will keep on falling.

#3 Japanese candles

Most traders incline toward utilizing the Japanese candle graphs since they are more clear and decipher. Traders utilize specific candle examples to identify trading openings.

Having a steady and secure swing trading plan is a standout amongst the most significant traps of the market. Accomplishment in the business sectors is, to a great extent, a matter of order. It is tied in with having the ideal arrangement. A characterized swing trading plan goes about as a manual to keeping one on a trading way to thriving. Absence of arranging in cash the executives has its expenses and outcomes. Things being what they are, for what reason do you need a trading plan? All things considered; it is a significant formula for progress wherein you can have it both ways. Try not to depend on excelling in the business sectors, if you don't plan to be beneficial. Here is a portion of the top reasons why swing traders need a trading plan.

SWING TRADING PLAN

1. Apathetic Thinking= Trouble

To turn into a reliably benefit making trader, you have to get over apathetic reasoning, which causes the extinguishing of trading accounts. Self-control is the way to achievement in the business sectors, and a nitty-gritty Swing trading plan will keep you on the correct way.

2. Plan= Accountability

Having a well-characterized trading plan implies that one considers oneself responsible for specific norms. This is basic for improving responsibility as a trader and positively affecting swing trading. The swing trading plan fills in as a token of the best advantages for your trading account at some random point in time. Be that as it may, in the wake of investigating the business sectors does not help either. The more you dissed factors in the market, the greater test it will posture to your trading account. To understand your total potential as a swing trader in the market, persistence is the key.

Rehashing the blast bust cycle of the market will arrive you in money related doldrums. Continuing without an arrangement resembles monetary suicide. The best remedy for passionate trading missteps is a very much idea out swing trading plan. This is on the grounds that the arrangement depicts blueprints in a given market situation in solid terms. A brilliant trading plan shouldn't be excessively confused, yet it needs to be efficient.

3. Trading= More Than Picking a Winning Number

Never liken trading with betting, on the grounds that the two are altogether different. It is critical to decide your entrance procedure. The passage point can have a significant effect between representing the moment of truth in trading. Regardless of whether you are reemerging toward a market pattern or setting off a moving normal, realize that arranging can assume a significant job in progress and disappointment.

4. Hazard Reward Analysis= Guarding Against Losses

The hazard to compensate situation on a potential trade set up before one enters it is a significant factor to consider. There ought to be lucidity in regards to the swing position estimating. Changing position measure while trading is basic for gathering the stop-misfortune separate. Going the other route round is essentially surrendering to voracity.

5. Exit Point= Clarity with respect to Strategy

One ought to be clear about the leave technique before entering the trade. This is the embodiment of fruitful trading. If you figure you will make sense of it as trading unfurls, be set up for stuns. When you are not in a trade, you are the target, and this is an ideal opportunity to set up your parameters.

6. Trading Plan=GPS for Trades

A trading plan has likewise been compared by specialists to a GPS gadget in that you enter where you need to proceed to check if the GPS has put you destined for success. Realizing when you've made an off-base turn, altering your developments with the goal that you can be pointed back the correct way…. these are a piece of having a trading plan.

A trading plan is much similar to a GPS in that it focuses you the correct way and causes you to accomplish steady benefit. It likewise encourages you to trade short your feelings and in addition to a ton of solace. Trading without much forethought includes depending on instinct and speculations, making it progressively about betting and less about managing in protections.

7. If You Fail to Plan, Then You've Already Planned to Fail

A trading plan is no certification of accomplishment. Be that as it may, a great trading plan will assist you with being a piece of the game longer than the individuals who don't have a trading plan. There are additionally numerous commonsense manners by which the trading plan will be useful to traders.

8. Great Trading Plan= Managing Risk Better

High or okay conveys unique importance. By putting a number to this, you can survey the precise degree to which this trade is hazardous. Hazard per trade scale could change contingent on your craving for taking risks and what you bring to the contributing table.

9. Setting up Strategies Beforehand= Less Stress, More Profits

Setting up section and leave methodologies in advance will lower pressure and make supports for making benefits. Enthusiastic reactions blemish chances at benefit; methodology stays at work past 40 hours. Build up certain section and leave criteria just as standards to stick to.

Graphs can be utilized to track market slants and considering passage or exit depends on target investigation instead of gut-level reasoning.

10. Savvy Trading Plan= Streamlined Decision Making

Money related markets move with stunning speed, and this is when trying not to be raced into ill-advised choices. Trading plans are a point of reference inside the circumstance fully expecting predicaments being confronted. Trading plans can remove the passionate remainder from the trading recipe. Already methodologies will survey the quality and rightness of your basic leadership process.

11. Trading Plan = Trading Diary

Think about your trading plan as a trading parcel or journal which you can use to follow every one of the trades and make notes concerning this achievement and disappointment. A trading log is a great instrument for taking a gander at the master plan, and you can get a fast perspective on the trading history and find slip-ups and blunders just as accomplishments in the bigger plan of things. For a depiction of the trading hits and misses, nothing beats a decent swing trading plan.

12. Proficient Trading Plan= Fewer Trading Mistakes

Trustworthiness and mindfulness are significant in the market. Consistent evaluation of hits and disappointments in the market will push you to reject slip-ups made in the past as well as embrace what works and simplify your trading choices.

13. Substantial Trading Plan= Maintaining Trading Discipline

A trading system can be a speedy token of the objectives and restrictions looked by a swing trader. The composed arrangement is useful for following your trading order and adhering to it will guarantee that there are no deviations of any sort.

14. Trading Plan= Every Good Swing Trader's Move

Who needs trading plans? Each great swing trader worth his time and energy do. From first time amateurs to prepared experts, trading plans are basic regardless of what sort of trades you need to climate. Profiting by a trading plan is choosing what is to your greatest advantage and doing it.

15. Trading Plan= Edge Over Other Traders

Without a decent trading arrangement, you are basically betting. It is essential to make a trading arrangement and stick to it else you will discover numerous diversions along the way. It is insightful to have an arrangement with the goal that you can become familiar with the required data about the market, getting data in regards to trading essentials and fundamental methodologies.

16. Successful Trading Plan= Knowledge of Results

A skillfully confined arrangement likewise gives a targeted criticism in regards to whether a specific technique for trading is working or not. You can likewise investigate why you're occupied with trading a specific stock and settling on educated choices as opposed to irregular oncs.

If you need to push your very own pontoon as opposed to paddle haphazardly in the waters, trading plans are basic.

17. Complete Plan= Comprehensive Research

Settling on irregular choices implies you come up short on the explanation for what you are doing, and this can't work in the business sectors. You need an edge, and a well-characterized plan can give you simply that. Along these lines, before making a trade, you have to concoct a decent trading arrangement.

When you know the greatest hazard, which can be taken per trade, you have to think of passage standards and specific value developments, diagram examples, insights and different pointers of the market's wellbeing at the season of diving in. Leave focuses incorporate value developments, diagram examples, pointers or inversions of the sign which prompted the passage. Different elements to consider are whether you will utilize trailing stops, participate in dynamic trade the board and diagram time period to which ways out would be connected. In this way, be clear about your purposes behind entering and leaving the swing market and have an arrangement for this with the goal that you don't become mixed up in the center!

HOW IT DIFFERS FROM OTHER TYPES OF TRADING AND WHERE IT IS APPLIED

Dynamic traders frequently bunch themselves into two camps: the informal investors and the swing traders. Both try to benefit from momentary stock developments (versus long haul ventures), however, which trading procedure is the better one? Here are the upsides and downsides of day trading as opposed to swing trading, and the real differences between the two.

Day trading, as the name proposes, includes making many trades in a solitary day, given specialized examination and advanced diagramming frameworks. The informal investor's goal is to bring home the bacon from trading stocks, wares, or monetary standards, by making little benefits on various trades and topping misfortunes on unrewarding trades. Informal investors regularly don't keep any positions or claim any protections medium-term.

Day trading includes a novel range of abilities that can be difficult to ace. Investopedia's Become a Day Trader course gives a top to the bottom outline of day trading, total with over five hours of on-request video. During the course, you will take in everything from request types to specialized examination methods to expand your balanced hazard returns.

Day Trading

The greatest draw of day trading is the potential for stupendous benefits. Be that as it may, this may just be a plausibility for the uncommon person who has every one of the attributes, for example, definitiveness, order, and persistence, required to turn into a fruitful informal investor.

The U.S. Protections and Exchange Commission (SEC) calls attention to that "days traders regularly endure budgetary misfortunes in their first long stretches of trading, and numerous never graduate to benefit making status." While the SEC alerts that informal investors should just hazard cash they can stand to lose; actually numerous informal investors acquire gigantic misfortunes on obtained monies, either through margined trades or capital obtained from family or different sources. These misfortunes may diminish their day trading vocation as well as place them in significant obligation.

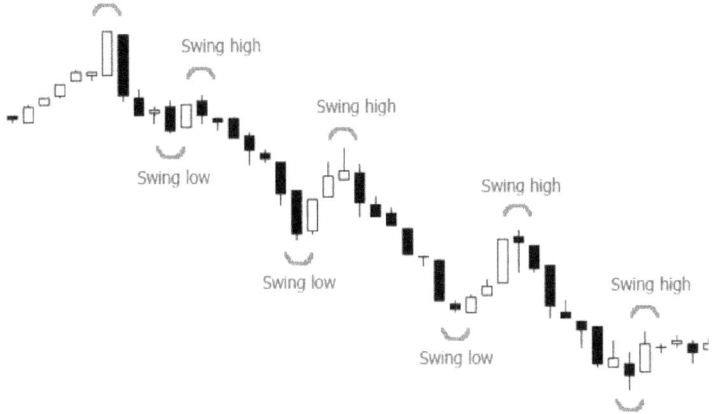

The informal investor works alone, free from the impulses of corporate fat cats. He can have an adaptable working timetable, get some much-needed rest whenever required, and work at his own pace, in contrast to somebody on the corporate treadmill.

Informal investors need to contend with high-recurrence traders, mutual funds, and other market experts who burn through millions to pick up trading favorable circumstances. In this condition, an informal investor has minimal decision however, to spend intensely on a trading stage, diagramming programming, cutting edge PCs, and so forth. Progressing costs incorporate expenses for getting live value statements and commission costs that can include on account of the volume of trades.

Long-lasting informal investors love the rush of setting their minds against the market and different experts

25

throughout each and every day. The adrenaline surge from fast flame trading is something very few traders will admit to, yet it is a major factor in their choice to bring home the bacon from trading. It's suspicious these sorts of individuals would be substance going through their days selling gadgets or poring over numbers in an office desk area.

To truly make a go at it, a trader must stop his normal everyday employment and surrender his relentless regularly scheduled check. From that point on, the informal investor must depend totally without anyone else expertise and endeavors to create enough benefit to pay the bills and appreciate a not too bad lifestyle.

Day trading is upsetting a direct result of the need to watch different screens to spot trading openings, and after that demonstration rapidly to abuse them. This must be done for a long time, and the necessity for such a high level of center and focus can frequently prompt burnout.

For some occupations in the fund, having the correct degree from the correct college is essential only for a meeting. Day trading, conversely, does not require costly instruction from an Ivy League school. While there are no formal instructive necessities for turning into an informal investor, courses in the specialized investigation and mechanized trading might be exceptionally useful.

Swing Trading

Swing trading depends on identifying swings in stocks, products, and monetary forms that happen over a time of days. A swing trade may take a couple of days to half a month to work out. In contrast to an informal investor, a swing trader isn't probably going to make trading a full-time profession.

Anybody with learning and speculation capital can have a go at swing trading. As a result of the more drawn out time allotment (from days to weeks rather than minutes to hours), a swing trader shouldn't be stuck to his PC screen throughout the day. He can even keep up a different all-day work (as long as he isn't checking trading screens all the time at work).

Trades by and large need time to work out. Keeping a trade for an advantage open for a couple of days or weeks may result in higher benefits than trading all through similar security on numerous occasions multi-day.

Since swing trading normally includes positions held at any rate medium-term, edge necessities are higher. Most extreme influence is normally multiple times one's capital. Contrast this and day trading where edges are multiple times one's capital.

The swing trader can set stop misfortunes. While there is a danger of a quit being executed at a negative value, it beats the consistent observing of every single vacant position that is an element of day trading.

Similarly, as with any style of trading, swing trading can likewise result in generous misfortunes. Since swing traders hold their situations for longer than informal investors, they additionally risk bigger misfortunes.

Since swing trading is only from time to time an all-day work, there is significantly less possibility of burnout because of stress. Swing traders typically have standard employment or another wellspring of salary from which they can balance or relieve trading misfortunes.

Swing trading should be possible with only one PC and ordinary trading instruments. It doesn't require the cutting-edge innovation of day trading.

Key Differences

Day trading and swing trading each have focal points and downsides. Neither one of the strategies is superior to the next, and traders ought to pick the methodology that works best for their aptitudes, inclinations, and lifestyle. Day trading is more qualified for people who are energetic about trading full time and have the three Ds: conclusiveness, control, and industriousness (requirements for effective day trading).

Day trading achievement likewise requires a propelled comprehension of specialized trading and diagramming. Since day trading is exceptional and distressing, traders ought to have the option to remain quiet and control their feelings enduring an onslaught. At last, day trading includes hazard—traders ought to be set up to once in a while leave with 100 percent misfortunes.

Swing trading, then again, does not require such an impressive arrangement of attributes. Since swing trading can be embraced by anybody with some speculation capital and does not require full-time consideration, it is a feasible alternative for traders who need to keep their all-day occupations, yet additionally, fiddle with the business sectors. Swing traders ought to likewise have the option to apply a mix of major and specialized examination, instead of specialized investigation alone.

THE MOST IMPORTANT THING: THE PRICE ACTION

Value activity for swing traders is the craft of seeing individual candles to decide the likely course of a stock - without utilizing any specialized markers.

Eventually, investigating value activity discloses to you who is responsible for a stock. It additionally reveals to you who is losing control: the purchasers or the vendors. When you can decide this, you can pinpoint inversions in stock and profit.

Become familiar with the value activity tips on this page, and I promise you that you will be a superior swing trader.

How about we start.

Tip #1. Identify backing and obstruction levels

This is an easy decision. Identifying backing and obstruction levels is one of the primary things you learn in the specialized investigation. It is the most significant part of diagram perusing. In any case, how many traders truly focus on it? Very few. Most are excessively bustling taking a gander at Stochastics, MACD, and other drivel.

A few traders feel that a help or obstruction level is a specific cost. Wrong. It's a territory on a stock diagram. Give me a chance to give you a model.

The zones that I have featured are the right help and obstruction levels. Frequently you will hear traders state something like this: "The help level for XYZ stock is $28.76." This isn't right. It's a zone - not a specific cost.

Tip #2. Break down swing focuses

Swing focuses (some call them "turn focuses") are those territories on a stock outline where significant momentary inversions happen. Be that as it may, not all swing focuses are made equivalent. In actuality, your choice to purchase a pullback will rely on the earlier swing point.

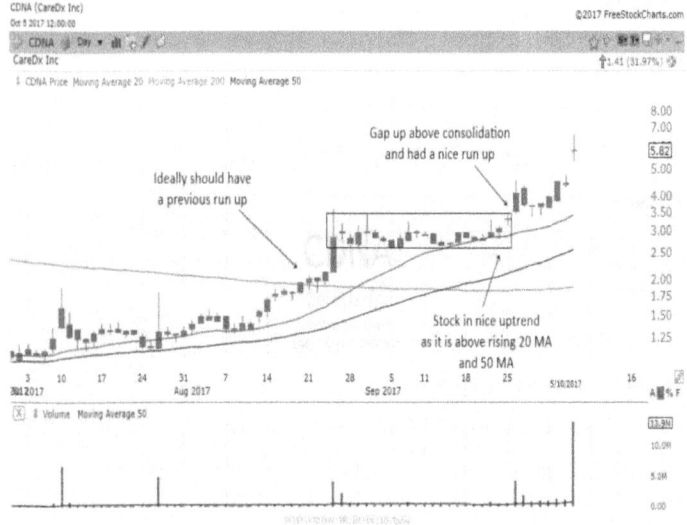

In the first place, there isn't much space to work with! The separation between the pullback and the earlier high is excessively little. You need more space to run with the goal that you can, at any rate, get your stop to make back the initial investment.

The subsequent issue is this: The earlier high (yellow region) is made out of a bunch of candles. This is a solid obstruction territory! Along these lines, it will be extremely difficult for a stock to get through this region. Rather, hope to trade pullbacks where the earlier high is just made out of a couple of candles.

Tip #3. Search for a wide range of candles

Wide range candles mark significant changes in notion on each outline - in each time span. They mark significant defining moments and can regularly be utilized to identify inversions.

This stock switched within earlier wide range candles. For what reason would a stock do this? Since the majority of the traders that passed up "the huge move" presently have another opportunity to get in. This purchasing weight causes inversion. Straightforward, huh?

Tip #4. Tight range candles lead to hazardous moves

Limited range candles can likewise disclose to you that an inversion is unavoidable. This low instability condition can prompt touchy moves.

Restricted range candles disclose to you that the past force has backed off. Purchasers and merchants are in balance, yet, in the long run, one of them will assume responsibility for the stock!

Tip #5. Discover rejected value levels

On candle outlines, lower or upper shadows on candles, as a rule, implies that there is a mallet candle design or a falling star candle design (if the shadow is long enough). Despite the name, these shadows mean a certain something: A value level has been rejected.

Envision what this sled flame resembled during the (prior day it turned into a mallet). It was extremely bearish! Be that as it may, sooner or later during the day, the bulls dismissed the lower value level. I can envision the bulls saying, "Hello, hold up an only a second. You bears have taken this excessively far. This stock is worth considerably more than the value that you moved it to."

What's more, the purchasing starts.

Tip #6. Become familiar with the half standard

How might you tell if a light is significant? Simple. Hope to perceive how far it has moved into the earlier days go. If it moves at any rate half into the earlier days run, then it is significant. What's more, it is particularly significant if it closes in any event half into the earlier days run. This generally appears on the stock outline as a piercing candle design or an immersing candle design.

The majority of the significant inversions in this stock happened simply after a flame moved at any rate half into the earlier days go (some moved substantially more than half).

This idea is powerful to the point that I am suspicious of purchasing any pullback except if it moves in any event half into the earlier days run.

Tip #7. The hole and trap value design

All holes are significant "tells" on any stock diagram. In any case, there is one sort of hole that is particularly significant when investigating value activity (and pinpointing inversions). This is known as a hole and trap. This is a stock that holes down at the open however then shuts the day over the opening cost.

You can likely observe what's going on here. The stock holes down at the open. Everybody thinks this stock is going to tank. Be that as it may, it doesn't! Purchasers come in and move this stock ideal back up. You can take a gander at one of these candles and nearly observe the majority of the confounded faces on other stock traders!

Tip #8. Measure the profundity of a swing

How far does a stock move into the earlier swing? More than midway or less? The response to these inquiries is significant in light of the fact that it can decide the future course of the stock.

The value activity moved mostly down (bolt) into the earlier swing (spotted line). This is great. If it remembered more than that, you might need to scrutinize the legitimacy of the move. This is because a stock in a solid pattern ought not to backtrack more than most of the way into an earlier swing. It should experience purchasing weight sooner than the midway imprint. Also, common stocks will invert directly at the midway imprint.

Tip #9. Back to back up days and continuous down days

Stocks will invert bearing after back to back up days or down days. Thus, it pays to remember this when you are hoping to purchase or short a stock.

You ought to dependably hope to short a stock after back to back up days. Also, you should hope to purchase a stock-after back to back down days. This is illogical for new traders since they will in general partner a stock going down as "terrible" (which means sell) and stock going up as "great" (which means purchase). Truth be told, it is the exact inverse!

Tip #10. Area of cost in a pattern

You have heard the truism, "The pattern is your companion." I state, "The start of a pattern is your companion!" That is because the absolute best moves happen at the earliest reference point of a pattern...

This stock broke out (even line) from a twofold base (circumnavigated). Another pattern has started. Along these lines, you need to purchase this stock on the primary pullback (bolt) after the breakout.

Along these lines, there you have it. These value activity tips and traps will profit in the securities exchange.

You can utilize this data to make your own trading methodologies and frameworks. The best part is that once you ace this craftsmanship, you will never need to depend on specialized markers again to settle on trading choices.

They won't be fundamental.

Value activity portrays the attributes of security's value developments. This development is frequently broken down for value changes in the ongoing past. In basic terms, value activity is a trading method that enables a trader to peruse the market and settle on emotional trading choices dependent on the ongoing and real value developments, instead of depending exclusively on specialized pointers.

Since it overlooks the basic examination factors and concentrates more on later and past value development, the value activity trading technique is subject to specialized investigation apparatuses.

[Many informal investors center around value activity trading methodologies to rapidly produce a benefit over a brief timeframe outline. For instance, they may search for a straightforward breakout from the session's high, go into a long position, and utilize exacting cash the board techniques to create a benefit. If you're keen on day trading, Investopedia's Become a Day Trader Course gives an exhaustive audit of the subject from an accomplished Wall Street trader. You'll learn demonstrated trading systems, hazard the executive's procedures, and substantially more in more than five hours of on-request video, activities, and intelligent substance.]

APPARATUSES USED FOR PRICE ACTION TRADING

Since value activity trading identifies with later recorded information and past value developments, all specialized examination apparatuses like graphs, pattern lines, value groups, high and low swings, specialized levels (of help, opposition, and union), and so forth are considered according to the trader's decision and system fit.

The apparatuses and examples seen by the trader can be straightforward value bars, value groups, break-outs, pattern lines, or complex blends including candles, instability, channels, and so forth.

Mental and social elucidations and ensuing activities, as chosen by the trader, likewise make up a significant part of value activity trades. For e.g., regardless of what occurs, if a stock floating at 580 crosses the by and by the set mental degree of 600, then the trader may expect a further upward move to take a long position. Different traders may have a contrary view – when 600 is hit, the individual accepts a value inversion and subsequently takes a short position.

No two traders will decipher a specific value activity similarly, as each will have his or her own translation, characterized rules, and different social comprehension of it. Then again, a specialized investigation situation (like 15

DMA traverse 50 DMA) will yield comparable conduct and activity (long position) from various traders.

Generally, value activity trading is a deliberate trading practice, supported by specialized examination devices and ongoing value history, where traders are allowed to take their very own choices inside an offered situation to take trading positions, according to their abstract, social and mental state.

WHO USES PRICE ACTION TRADING?

Since value activity trading is a way to deal with value forecasts and hypothesis, it is utilized by retail traders, examiners, arbitrageurs, and notwithstanding trading firms who utilize traders. It tends to be utilized on a wide scope of protections, including values, bonds, swing, items, subsidiaries, and so forth.

Value Action Trading Steps

Most experienced traders following value activity trading keep various choices for perceiving trading examples, passage and leave levels, stop-misfortunes, and related perceptions. Having only one procedure on one (or different) stocks may not offer adequate trading openings. Most situations include a two-advance procedure:

1. Identifying a situation: Like a stock cost getting into a bull/bear stage, the channel goes, breakout, and so on.

2. Within the situation, identifying trading openings: Like once stock is in a bull run, is it prone to (an) overshoot or (b) retreat. This is a totally emotional decision and can fluctuate from one trader to the next, even given the equivalent indistinguishable situation.

41

Here are a couple of models:

1) A stock achieves its high according to the trader's view and after that retreats to a marginally lower level (situation met). The trader would then be able to choose whether the person in question supposes it will frame a twofold top to go higher or drop further after a mean inversion.

2) The trader sets a story and roof at a specific stock cost dependent on the supposition of low unpredictability and no breakouts. If the stock value lies in this range (situation met), the trader can take positions accepting the set floor/roof going about as help/obstruction levels, or take another view that the stock will breakout in either heading.

3) A characterized breakout situation being met and after that trading opportunity existing regarding breakout continuation (going further a similar way) or breakout pull-back (coming back to the past level)

As can be seen, value activity trading is firmly helped by specialized investigation instruments. However, the last trading call is reliant on the individual trader, offering the person in question adaptability as opposed to upholding an exacting arrangement of guidelines to be pursued.

THE POPULARITY OF PRICE ACTION TRADING

Value activity trading is more qualified for short-to-medium term restricted benefit trades, rather than long haul speculations.

Most traders accept that the market pursues an arbitrary example, and there is no reasonable methodical approach to characterize a technique that will dependably work. By joining the specialized examination apparatuses with the ongoing value history to identify trade openings dependent on the trader's very own understanding, value activity trading has a great deal of help in the trading network.

MARKET PSYCHOLOGY FOR SWING TRADING

The brain research behind trading stocks is the power that moves the securities exchange. A stock graph is just an image of human feelings. Painted on the canvas are the feelings of voracity, dread, expectation, and rapture. As a trained trader, you gain by the mental evil presences that plague different traders.

- Should I purchase?

- Should I sell?

- Should I take benefits?

- Should I assume a misfortune?

These are a portion of the inquiries that decimate trading accounts because the learner traders posing these inquiries don't have an arrangement. If you solicited an expert trader one from these inquiries, the individual in question would state, "I don't have the foggiest idea. What does your arrangement guide you to do."?

So, what winds up occurring? They get energized and purchase best case scenario conceivable time. Then the stock inverts. Dread sneaks i, and after that, the stock goes lower... what's more, lower... what's more, lower. At long last, the torment turns out to be an excessive amount to manage, so they sell assuming a gigantic misfortune.

You can't take huge misfortunes and hope to be a beneficial swing trader, and if you can't assume a little misfortune, then you will take the mother all things considered! Trust it!

Presently we should take a gander at the brain science behind what happens when a stock goes in the ideal course:

Energy! Elation! Better believe it, I'm profiting! "I would be wise to offer to secure these benefits since I have had a few losing trades in succession." The trader then winds up selling too early!

At this point, I'm certain that you have heard the expression, "Keep your misfortunes little and let your champs run." Take a gander at what simply occurred in the above model. The un-trained trader has quite recently done the inverse! They have given their misfortunes a chance to get enormous, and they have restricted their victors!

The majority of this psychological anguish can be disposed of by having a conventional trading methodology and the psychological control to stay with it. Record an arrangement for the trade before you trade the stock. Then trade it as per the arrangement that you have composed. Keep in mind that you had concocted an arrangement before you got into the trade when your feelings were steady. Presently you can trade your arrangement with certainty.

For most learner traders, it isn't their technique that is making them lose cash. It is themselves that is their greatest adversary.

Figuring out how to trade stocks and applying specialized examination to diagrams is for the most part about human brain science - not outline examples and candle designs themselves. You need to comprehend the brain research behind these examples.

Here is a breakdown of what occurs:

Breakout Traders - These traders purchased the breakout. They work under the "more prominent trick hypothesis." They are simply asking that different traders tag along and purchase higher than they.

Learner Traders - These traders simply have no clue what they are doing. There are purchasing portions of stock that the breakout traders are presently offering to them.

Energy Traders - These traders are purchasing the pullback and will in general purchase close to the 10 MA. They are likely going to put their stop underneath the low of the sled.

Swing Traders - This is the place we come in. The stock falls beneath that mallet, and the force traders get ceased out. At this point, the vast majority of the learner traders and force traders have sold. Perceive how the volume has decreased? Past opposition currently moves toward becoming help.

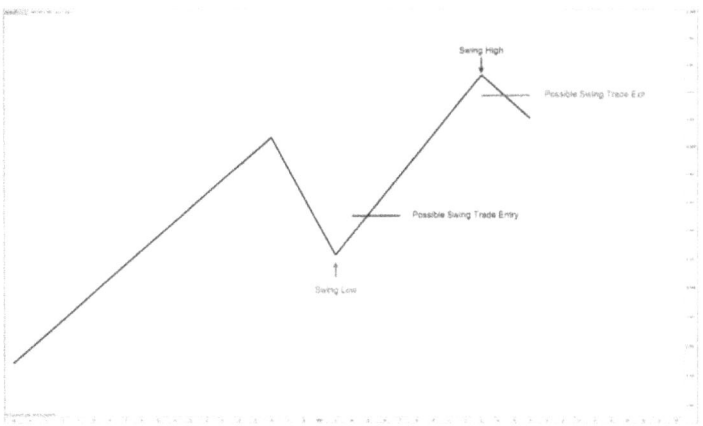

Fledgling Traders - once more, the learner traders are purchasing even under the least favorable conditions conceivable time. We need these traders with the goal that we can offer our offers to them and make a benefit.

This occurs over, and over, and over again - on each stock diagram in each time period.

Keep in mind this is all equitable hypothesis. We clearly wouldn't fret perusers - yet we can see how different traders think. How would I know this? Since I used to be a breakout trader... also, I used to be a learner trader... furthermore, I used to be an energy trader!

So, I have a general thought of how they think, where their stops are, and what they may do straightaway.

As swing traders, all we truly need to know is the brain science behind the moves in the securities exchange. We need to figure out how to control our own feelings first, and afterward, we need to figure out how to benefit off of those that have not figured out how to control them!

EMOTIONS: THE REASON WHY MOST PEOPLE LOSE MONEY BY OPERATING ON THE FINANCIAL MARKETS AND HOW TO AVOID IT

A commonly known fact is that most swing traders fail. In fact, it is estimated that 96 percent of swing traders lose cash and end up stopping. The swing site DailyFX found that many swing traders show improvement over that, yet new traders still have extreme planning making progress in this market. To enable you to make it into that tricky 4 percent of winning traders, the accompanying rundown demonstrates to you probably the most well-known reasons why swing traders lose cash.

Get to know the Market

The market isn't something you beat, yet something you comprehend and join when a pattern is characterized. In the meantime, the market is something that can shake you out if you are attempting to get a lot from it with excessively minimal capital. Having the "beating the market" outlook regularly makes traders trade too forcefully or conflict with patterns, which is a certain catastrophe waiting to happen.

Low Start-Up Capital

Most cash traders begin searching for an approach to escape obligation or to profit. It is basic for swing advertisers to urge you to trade huge part sizes and trade utilizing a strong influence to create enormous profits for a limited quantity of beginning capital.

You should have some cash to profit, and it is feasible for you to create exceptional profits for constrained capital temporarily. Nonetheless, with just a limited quantity of capital and outsized hazard due to too-high influence, you will end up being passionate with each swing of the market's good and bad times and hopping in and out and the most noticeably awful occasions conceivable.

You can resolve this issue by never trading with a too-modest quantity of capital. This is a difficult issue to get around for somebody that needs to begin trading on a shoestring. $1,000 is sensible to add up to begin off with if you trade little (miniaturized scale parcels or littler). Else, you are simply setting yourself up for a potential debacle.

Inability to Manage Risk

Hazard the board is critical to survival as a swing trader as in life. You can be a talented trader and still be cleared out by poor hazard the executives. Your main employment isn't to make a benefit, yet rather to secure what you have. As your capital gets exhausted, your capacity to make a benefit is lost.

To balance this danger and actualize great hazard the board, put in stop-misfortune requests and move them once you have a sensible benefit. Use parcel sizes that are sensible contrasted with your record capital. The greater part of all, if a trade never again bodes well, receive in return.

Yielding to Greed

A few traders feel that they have to crush each and every pip out of a move in the market. There is cash to be made in the swing markets each day. Attempting to snatch each and every pip before a money pair turns can make you hold positions excessively long and set you up to lose the productive trade that you are trading.

The arrangement appears glaringly evident here, simply don't be ravenous. It's fine to go for a sensible benefit; however, there are a lot of pips to go around. Monetary standards keep on moving each day, so there is no compelling reason to get that last pip; the following open door is directly around the bend.

Uncertain Trading

Now and again, you may wind up experiencing trading regret. This happens when a trade that you open isn't quickly productive, and you begin saying to yourself that you picked a misguided course. Then you close your trade and turn around it, just to see the market return the underlying way that you picked.

For this situation, you have to pick a bearing and stay with it. All that is exchanging forward and backward will simply make you consistently lose little bits of your record at once until your contributing capital is drained.

Attempting to Pick Tops or Bottoms

Numerous new traders attempt to pick defining moments in cash sets. They will put a trade on a couple, and as it props up off course, they keep on adding to their position being certain that it is going to pivot this time. If you trade like this, at last, you end up with substantially more presentation than you arranged, alongside a horribly negative trade.

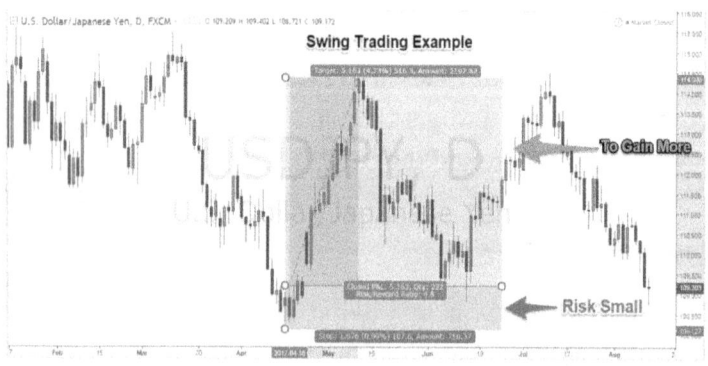

It's ideal to trade with the pattern. It's not worth the boasting rights to realize that you selected base effectively from 10 endeavors. If you think the pattern is going to change, and you need to take a trade the new conceivable way, hang tight for an affirmation on the pattern change.

If you need to get a situation at the base, get the base in an upturn, not in a downtrend. If you need to open a situation at the top, pick a top when the market's creation a remedial move higher, not an upswing that is a piece of a bigger a downtrend.

Declining to Be Wrong

A few trades simply don't work out. It is human instinct to need to be correct, however now and then you simply aren't. As a trader, you simply need to acknowledge that you're off-base here and there and proceed onward, rather than sticking to being correct and winding up with a zero-balance trading account.

It is a difficult activity, however once in a while, you simply need to concede that you committed an error. It is possible that you entered the trade for the off-base reasons, or it simply didn't work out how you arranged it. In any case, the best activity is simply conceding the slip-up, dump the trade, and proceed onward to the following chance.

Purchasing a System

There are some supposed swing trading frameworks available to be purchased on the web. A few traders are out there searching for the ever-subtle 100-percent precise swing trading framework. They continue purchasing frameworks and attempting them until at last quitting any pretense of, choosing that there is no real way to win.

As another trader, you should acknowledge that there is no such thing as a free lunch. Succeeding at swing trading takes work simply like whatever else. You can discover accomplishment by structure your very own technique, procedure, and framework as opposed to purchasing useless frameworks on the web from not exactly trustworthy advertisers.

Realize why most traders lose cash, and why that will dependably be the situation. It's a deliberate necessity of the market. While people can part from the group and make better than expected returns, by far most of the individuals will proceed to purchase and sell at the off-base occasions. Gain from the mix-ups of the crowd, so you can venture into the little gathering of reliably fruitful traders.

This book is separated into segments:

- How patterns and inversions occur, which is deliberate of significant misfortunes by the group.

- The social impact factor that shapes the group and baits individuals into the failure's circle.

- The numbers game: the best traders constantly take the cash of the less experienced.

- How to part from the group and become a free and reliably productive trader.

Most traders have heard the measurements "95% of traders lose cash" or "Just a couple of percent of traders bring home the bacon at it."

While the numbers differ marginally from concentrate to examine, the truth of the matter is numerous traders will lose cash, and it can't be maintained a strategic distance from. A wide range of reasons is given for the misfortunes, including poor cash the board, terrible planning, or a poor procedure. These variables do assume a job in individual trading achievement… however, there is a more profound motivation behind why a great many people lose.

Most traders will lose paying little heed to what techniques they utilize. Regardless of whether all traders knew how (remember, knowing, and doing are two altogether different things) to trade effectively dependent on current conditions, most traders would, in any case, lose as time goes on. We should investigate why that is.

Value Extremes Require Nearly Everyone to Get Onboard

To comprehend why most traders, lose, we have to see how costs move. We additionally need to consider the enormous number of individuals who get included right when the cost is going to turn. This is the place the mass misfortunes occur.

When a purchasing free for all grabs hold in a market, it's difficult to see the development for what it is: something that will pass! Everything passes. However, at the time, individuals see other individuals purchasing, which makes them believe that if they purchase now, then other individuals will purchase after them. Whenever you make a theoretical buy, you are doing as such in light of the fact that you accept other individuals will purchase after you, pushing the cost up which enables you to sell for a benefit.

Costs possibly rise if a greater number of individuals are venturing in to purchase that are happy to sell. While we can do a wide range of extravagant examination and make estimates about value, all we are truly doing is making a wagered that individuals will venture in to purchase or sell. We are examining individuals since it is individuals that purchase and sell and cause costs to move. Furthermore, it's kin who cause rehashing designs, that we can trade off of, in the money related markets.

Subsequently, an upturn is made by an ever increasing number of individuals proceeding to drive the cost up. A cost can't go up some other way… individuals should be happy to pay ever more elevated costs. In the long run, there are no more individuals who are eager to purchase at more expensive rates, or there are a larger number of individuals willing to sell than purchase. The general population who purchased close to the top are left holding the misfortunes.

One major issue is that countless individuals get included appropriate close to the top. For instance, stock has been ascending for a long time, and as more individuals get some answers concerning it, they begin heaping in. In any case, there is just a predetermined number of individuals who care about that stock and are happy to get it. When the majority have heaped in, there is nobody else to purchase and the general population who purchased before in the pattern begin to sell, which then alarms the general population who purchased late in the pattern, and the domino impact starts cutting costs down.

We should look at a model: Bitcoin. Bitcoin had been rising relentlessly somewhere in the range of 2016 and 2017, however with not a ton of enthusiasm from the overall population. Close to the center of 2017, significantly more individuals wound up intrigued. We can see this by what number of individuals Googled "bitcoin." We can accept that individuals scanning for data on an item are not specialists, but instead need to find out about it. The diagram demonstrates that there was a blast in enthusiasm, bringing an entirely different cluster of purchasers into Bitcoin.

Notice how the number of individuals looking for "bitcoin" harmonized with the cost of bitcoin cresting. An entire heap of individuals who had never known about bitcoin ended up keen on it, helped fuel the rally, however then ubiquity hit its minimum amount significance there was nobody left to purchase. By a wide margin, interest was the most noteworthy close to the top. While canny financial specialists made cash off this purchasing free for all, the majority who made the purchasing craze (and the information demonstrates they purchased at the top), lost a great deal of cash.

Maintaining a strategic distance from mass misfortunes, and making benefits as an individual, will be talked about later on. For the time being, my point is to demonstrate that the vast majority get included close defining moments. Which means most people lose, and are in reality the impetus for turning the market the other way. There is a point of confinement to everything, and the mass furor makes that cutoff be hit.

En route up, there will be a lot of individuals who would prefer not to get included in light of the fact that they accept the cost is as of now excessively high. In any case, the market continues ticking higher; thus, a couple of the stragglers participate and purchase. Some still hold out, and the market continues ticking higher. At long last, 85% of the populace is bullish, and there are still a few stragglers... and the market props up. Individuals are broadcasting their accomplishments and reciting that blast, and bust cycles are a relic of past times. At last, essentially every individual who could possibly purchase is currently in... and market dives the other way.

The market is probably not going to switch to any significant degree until nearly everybody is on one side.

Which means nearly everybody who joined that gathering late will lose. A lot of individuals may simply choose to pause; however, so will the market. Furthermore, if individuals are isolated, then the market will move in an extending style.

Individuals are the impetus. Without an enormous number of individuals to make an outrageous, the market won't hit an extraordinary and turn around. At the end of the day, the blast and bust cycles will never end. At any rate not as long as our business sectors are a lose-lose situation (more on that somewhat later on).

Endeavoring to enact the blast and bust cycles away is simply political pandering. Enormous upturns and downtrends are fundamental. You don't have one without the other.

Until nearly everybody who is watching that time period, and has the capacity and enthusiasm to trade it–is in the pattern, it won't stop. The pattern will continue onward, luring more individuals in. When it achieves the minimum amount, which it can't manage without basically everybody ready, an inversion happens.

Shockingly, the inconveniences are not over the normal individual. Not exclusively are a great many people given the shaft at the top, they additionally will in general frenzy out and sell at market bottoms. Their capitulation offering implies there is nobody left to sell, so not long after the value begins rising.

When the viewpoint is most grim, because everybody you know is losing cash and all you see on TV is how terrible the business sectors are, there is a solid motivator to sell and pursue the group. Indeed, the group settles on a poor choice, which it can't resist doing, and the market turns the other way.

The models are simply intended to demonstrate that the vast majority lose by acting in mass in the meantime. The majority can't maintain a strategic distance from it since it is there an activity that depletes the pattern and turns around it.

Despite the fact that a long-haul outline of the securities exchange demonstrates the cost of stocks rising, recall that the vast majority of the general population are flushed out in light of the fact that they are purchasing close pinnacles and selling close bottoms. Additionally, those long-haul graphs of the financial exchange, similar to the S&P 500 record, to exclude the stocks that have failed or fallen on harsh occasions. The S&P 500 just incorporates top organizations. If an organization starts losing cash, it is dropped from the file and along these lines has no negative impact on it. Obviously that stock still exists and if it performs, ineffectively individuals will lose cash.

WHY MOST TRADERS LOSE MONEY – SOCIAL INFLUENCE

Fruitful traders discover something that works and stick to it, not giving others a chance to pull them far from their system. This is the place ineffective traders turn out badly and why the group lose cash. In spite of a great many people's earnest attempts, they can't pull themselves far from the group when it truly checks.

When all you get notification from your companions and the media is how great this advantage is getting along, or how awful that benefit is getting along, it's difficult to take a contrarian to see. As people, we will, in general default to accessibility predisposition, which is accepting what we hear regularly.

If you make a wager against every other person and you are incorrect, your companions giggle at you, or you feel timid. You experience lament for passing up a major opportunity while others benefit (regardless of whether just incidentally).

There is a social expense to not being a piece of the group. You can't discuss trades with others, or you have to step cautiously on the grounds that the vast majority won't hold your view. If you do take a contrary view to the group, and you are correct, individuals may detest you since you profited while they lost their shirt. Sound absurd?

Consider the open hubbub during the Occupy Wall Street dissents, or individuals feeling incredible disdain for the multifaceted investments and traders that made billions by observing the lodging value breakdown and exploiting it! Or on the other hand, the director who is hated for keeping his activity while a few of his representatives are laid off.

Winning traders are frequently "crucified" during real market turns when the larger part lose. Individuals lean toward similarly invested organization, regardless of whether they talk their direction right to the poor house.

I recall that I had various radio meetings planned for 2008 to examine winning methodologies and benefitting from declining costs. The meetings were dropped because the hosts and makers contemplated profiting during a securities exchange crash was excessively fiery of a point!

It is anything but difficult to state, "I will pursue the group and get out before them." Following through on that is very difficult… which is the reason groups move together. Everybody in the group feels that. Likewise, if you get an offer and ask costs when individuals begin to sell, there are just such a large number of offers are each value level. Thus, if you need to get out you have to offer to lower offer value, then a lower one, then a lower one. Everybody can't get out at a decent cost… just the fastest and most experienced commonly get out before genuine harm is finished.

Everybody decides to be an individual and trade their own particular manner, and by doing as such most end up being with the group that loses cash. Why? Since every individual lets it happen unwittingly. Their social state of mind, whether it be confidence, avarice, dread, and so forth. – is likely being powered by a similar social temperament common in the public arena. It is no mix-up that people start to like similar sorts of designs that everybody is wearing.

In a mission to change, most of society winds up evolving together, moving towards comparative wants and far from comparable aversions. In this way, what the market is putting forth gives the precise thing that will draw the trader into the group.

Consider why the spike in bitcoin was so charming? Individuals thought they were acting mindfully by becoming tied up with another innovation that would change the world, much the same as in the Dotcom bubble. They thought $15,000 to $20,000 per coin was shabby because it would quickly rise to $100,000. Such thoughts were normal in the media at the time. The data that made individuals think they were making an incredible trade was being sustained to them by the group who accepted something very similar. Huge numbers of these individuals were not acting freely, even though they thought they were. They every single joined power, crowded and drove the cost up. In any case, nobody ventured in after them, and the cost dipped under $7,000. While the cost may go up or down, later on, that doesn't change the way that the greatest number of individuals were tricked in near the top and will sell close to a base.

Regardless of what the market is, when something gets extremely hot or cold, we are bound to see and find out about it from our companions, through advertisements, and on the news. In this condition there will be heaps of "assistance" to invite us into the group, instruct us to be a piece of the group, and start us into the universe of the clueless leaders and their even more clueless followers.

WHY MOST TRADERS LOSE MONEY – A NUMBERS GAME

Budgetary pundits will make explanations, for example, "Most expert cash supervisors can't beat the S&P 500 benchmark." True. In any case, it isn't the expert cash supervisor demonstrating their obliviousness, it is these pundits who see nothing about market developments.

Most market development is made by expert cash directors who are overseeing trillions of dollars in resources, and furthermore by different experts/organizations who need to execute or support dangers to do their business. In this way, if the market is up 10% in a year, it is on the grounds that these expert store chiefs have by and large purchased the market up 10%. In this way, it is outlandish for most expert cash administrators to make over 10% that year since it is identical to requesting that somebody beat them self at a round of tennis.

Returns will be spread out from negative comes back to significantly increase digit returns, however, all things considered, they will have made about 10%, short an administration charge, and costs which means most reserve directors will fail to meet expectations. If the market is up 10%, the normal fence investments return might be in the ballpark of 8 to 9% after charges, perhaps lower.

Most of financial specialists and traders won't beat the benchmark since they themselves make and are a piece of that benchmark!

Is truly fascinating that while extraordinary speculative stock investments may make a normal of 20%/year in the course of the most recent 20 years, the normal financial specialist in that reserve has a high likelihood of making far not as much as that. Why? Since they contribute and haul out their assets at the off-base focuses, much the same as they do in the market. The fence investments or shared reserve is a (smaller scale) showcase, where speculators/traders can store and pull back dependent on how they figure the reserve will do.

Certain traders do figure out how to beat reliably. Numerous different traders and amateur financial specialists go to the business sectors with a bunch of bills and afterward lose it. There is a relentless and ceaseless stream of these individuals. They feed the kitties of those traders that are effective. Likewise, the very certainty that such a significant number of individuals heap into (out of) showcase tops (bottoms) implies there are good open doors for those that can watch out for the market.

All together for the brilliance stories to happen, for example, traders making a 100%. 500%… 2000% returns (regardless of whether in one day, one year or quite a while)– what number of traders must lose their shirt (or surrender benefits) for that to occur? Parts! Take a gander at it a different way. That informal investor that made $6,000,000 a year ago got that cash from someplace. Since little retail traders make most out of the absolute number of traders (high in number, little in worth contrasted with experts) all things considered, $6,000,000 was taken ideal from those retail traders a few thousand dollars at any given moment.

For an informal investor to make $6,000,000 in a year, that implies around 120 individuals lost $50,000 each and additionally surrendered $50,000 each in potential benefit! Or on the other hand, 1200 individuals lost $5,000. This is a simplified model. However, it provides a point of view not regularly considered. With the goal for somebody to win, another person must lose or surrender benefit.

The huge returns that bait individuals by the thousand to the business sectors are unexpectedly what make huge returns for other people and misfortunes to the droves.

As Individuals Apart from the Crowd

The group isn't a group until most are included.

Groups can't make solid patterns until most are included.

A pattern won't stop until about everybody is ready for the group.

When everybody is ready, it turns around.

Since the group can't win, that implies just a little level of people can.

While this article gives a wide setting, it applies to the little scale also. Informal investors get captured in similar group conduct without knowing it. That rising stock they observe throughout the morning before at last hopping in, just to have it move the other way, is a similar wonder on a little scale. On a 1-minute outline, when the upturn turns around, there is no out there right then and there who needs to purchase. Thus, the value inverts.

Purchasers and vendors can get depleted or elated on untouched edges. They experience short or potentially long blasts of feeling which result in short and long-haul activities/responses, all prompting examples which are obvious on unequaled casings. There are likewise degrees of bullishness and bearishness crosswise overtime allotments, which means on occasion the patterns and inversions will be forceful and at different occasions increasingly quiet contingent upon what number of traders (and people in general) are included.

Most importantly, traders must adhere to a well-characterized plan and trade that arrangement, notwithstanding it awkwardness. Most by far of the populace, and consequently by far most of traders, clasp under this awkward weight… a similar way we go after the chocolate bar rather than the carrots.

Since a large portion of the populace is glad to join the group, by having order joined with a fair procedure, it is conceivable to be one of only a handful couple of fruitful traders who doesn't participate in the group's losing ways. Informal investors, swing traders, and financial specialists can make incredible returns, however just if they cling to a couple of ideas.

If you don't have a clue what you are doing, purchase a file store and clutch it. Try not to attempt to trade. Over numerous years the market will, in general ascent, so this is a decent methodology for somebody with little experience or time to figure out how to trade appropriately. It sounds so basic, but most by far of individuals get scared or euphoric and purchase or sell it at the off-base time, therefore wrecking the long-haul returns.

For the individuals who effectively need to trade, don't be tricked into the group. Think autonomously, which means doing your own examination. Take a gander at diagrams and perceive how costs responded to different occasions and value designs. Create or learn systems for exploiting normal value designs. You don't should be correct constantly, regardless of whether an example just works out half of the time, yet you make more on champs than you lose on washouts, that is a triumphant example.

In making your very own trades dependent on your own exploration and methodologies you will some of the time be lined up with the group, and at times you won't.

However, it doesn't make a difference. You're trading your own game, given insights you know and trust from doing your examination and testing your system.

When you have a strategy, turn off the TV, discussions, and other's conclusions of the market. Their supposition depends on their methodology (if they have one!), not yours. You have taken the necessary steps without anyone else systems, so trust them.

Everybody comes to trading saying they will be superior to every other person, or that they simply need a little taste of the benefits and they will be glad. In any case, to make cash reliably implies you need be in the main couple of percent on the planet. Being in the main couple of percent of anything isn't simple. Be that as it may, it can really be as basic as purchasing and holding record support for a moderate gathering of benefits. That will put you in front of a great deal of support stock investments speculators. Or then again, if you need higher returns which are absolutely conceivable, it includes creating or learning methodologies and after that placing them into training all the more effectively (see above).

Trading is a procedure of nonstop control. We are just in the same class as our order. We can be an incredible trader one day, and extremely poor the following if we quit following our arrangement. Numerous individuals believe that once they become productive, they can unwind. Do you see proficient competitors simplicity off once they make it to the NBA, NHL or the PGA? No, they keep on buckling down at what they do... or they fall by the wayside.

The ones who last appreciate it. They appreciate the test and the challenge. The individuals who love trading will put in hours without night pondering it. The individuals who just trade to make a snappy buck will always be unable to contend with the individual who adores it and drenches themselves during the time spent learning and improving. Possibly trade if you truly need to. Without that enthusiasm, you are at a colossal disservice to the general population who have it.

Good karma on the voyage. While I believe it's imperative to clarify things, so individuals comprehend what they are getting into, I am obviously a trader myself. I began trading full time in 2005, adore it, and would prefer not to do whatever else. I put in a great deal of time to wind up productive and still put in a ton of time to keep up that exhibition and attempt to improve. I do accept that anybody with time, commitment, and some capital can be effective at trading. While a great many people will lose, as people, we have a decision with respect to how hard we will function. There is loads of capital out there drifting around, which we can figure out how to get. However, it won't occur by consistently doing what the group does.

MONEY AND RISK MANAGEMENT FOR SWING TRADING

Hazard the executives helps chop down misfortunes. It can likewise help shield a trader's record from losing the majority of his or her cash. The hazard happens when the trader endures a misfortune. If it tends to be overseen it, the trader can open oneself up to profiting in the market.

It is a basic, however, regularly ignored essential to effective dynamic trading. All things considered; a trader who has produced generous benefits can lose it all in only a couple of awful trades without a legitimate hazard the board methodology. So how would you build up the best strategies to check the dangers of the market?

This article will talk about some straightforward methodologies that can be utilized to ensure your trading benefits.

Arranging Your Trades

As Chinese military general Sun Tzu's broadly stated: "Each fight is won before it is battled." This expression suggests that arranging and system – not the fights – win wars. Also, fruitful traders regularly quote the expression: "Plan the trade and trade the arrangement." Just like in war, preparing can frequently mean the difference between progress and disappointment.

To start with, ensure your dealer is directly for continuous trading. A few dealers take into account clients who trade inconsistently. They charge high commissions and don't offer the privilege investigative instruments for dynamic traders.

Stop-misfortune (S/L) and take-benefit (T/P) focuses speak to two key manners by which traders can prepare when trading. Fruitful traders recognize what value they are happy to pay and at what value they are eager to sell. They would then be able to quantify the subsequent returns against the likelihood of the stock hitting their objectives. If the balanced return is sufficiently high, they execute the trade.

Then again, ineffective traders regularly enter a trade without having any thought of the focuses at which they will sell at a benefit or a misfortune. Like players on a fortunate — or unfortunate streak — feelings start to dominate and direct their trades. Misfortunes regularly incite individuals to hang on and want to make their cash back, while benefits can lure traders to hastily hang on for much more gains.

Consider the One-Percent Rule

A lot of informal investors pursue what's known as the one-percent rule. Essentially, this standard proposes that you should never put over 1% of your capital or your trading account into a solitary trade. So, if you have $10,000 in your trading account, your situation in some random instrument shouldn't be more than $100.

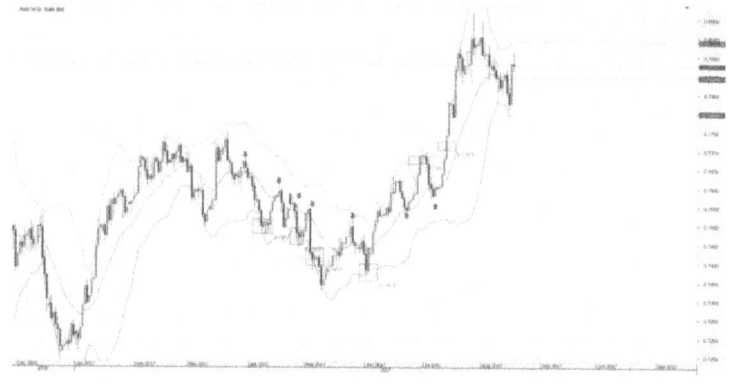

This technique is normal for traders who have records of under $100,000 — some even go as high as 2% if they can bear the cost of it. Numerous traders whose records have higher adjust may go with a lower rate. That is on the grounds that as the size of your record increments, so too does the position. The ideal approach to hold your misfortunes under tight restraints is to keep the standard beneath 2% — anymore, and you'd chance a considerable measure of your trading account.

Stop-Loss and Take-Profit Points

A stop-misfortune point is a cost at which a trader will sell a stock and write off the trade. This frequently happens when a trade does not work out how a trader is trusted. The focuses are intended to forestall the "it will return" attitude and farthest point misfortunes before they raise. For instance, if a stock breaks underneath a key help level, traders regularly sell as quickly as time permits.

Then again, a take-benefit point is the cost at which a trader will sell a stock and take a benefit on the trade. This is when the extra upside is constrained, given the dangers. For instance, if a stock is moving toward a key obstruction level after a huge move upward, traders might need to sell before the time of solidification happens.

Step by step instructions to Effectively Set Stop-Loss Points

Setting stop-misfortune and take-benefit focus are regularly done utilizing specialized investigation; the however crucial examination can likewise assume a key job in timing. For instance, if a trader is holding stock in front of income as fervor constructs, the individual in question might need to sell before the news hits the market if desires have turned out to be excessively high, paying little mind to whether the take-benefit cost has been hit.

Moving midpoints speak to the most well-known approach to set these focuses, as they are anything but difficult to figure and generally followed by the market. Key moving midpoints incorporate the 5-, 9-, 20-, 50-, 100-and 200-day midpoints. These are best set by applying them to a stock's diagram and deciding if the stock cost has responded to them in the past as either a help or obstruction level.

Another incredible method to place stop-misfortune or take-benefit levels is on help or opposition pattern lines. These can be drawn by associating past highs or lows that happened on significant, better than expected volume. Like with moving midpoints, the key is deciding levels at which the value responds to the pattern lines and, obviously, on high volume.

When setting these focuses, here are some key contemplations:

- Use longer-term moving midpoints for progressively unstable stocks to diminish the opportunity that a good for nothing value swing will trigger a stop-misfortune request to be executed.

- Adjust the moving midpoints to match the target value ranges. For instance, longer targets should utilize bigger moving midpoints to diminish the quantity of sign produced.

- Stop misfortunes ought not to be nearer than 1.5-times the present high-to-low range (instability), as it is too liable to even consider getting executed without reason.

- Adjust the stop misfortune as indicated by the market's unpredictability. If the stock cost isn't moving excessively, then the stop-misfortune focuses can be fixed.

- Use referred to major occasions, for example, income discharges, as key timespans to be in or out of a trade as unpredictability and vulnerability can rise.

Computing Expected Return

Setting stop-misfortune and take-benefit focuses are likewise important to ascertain the normal return. The significance of this count can't be exaggerated, as it powers traders to thoroughly consider their trades and support them. Also, it gives them an orderly method to look at different trades and select just the most productive ones.

This can be determined by utilizing the accompanying equation:

[(Probability of Gain) x (Take Profit % Gain)] + [(Probability of Loss) x (Stop-Loss % Loss)]

The consequence of this computation is a normal return for the dynamic trader, who will then quantify it against different chances to figure out which stocks to trade. The likelihood of addition or misfortune can be determined by utilizing verifiable breakouts and breakdowns from the help or obstruction levels — or for experienced traders, by making an informed theory.

Diversify and Hedge

Ensuring you take advantage of your trading implies never putting your eggs in a single container. If you put all your cash in one stock or one instrument, you're setting yourself up for a major misfortune. So, make sure to diversify your speculations. In addition to the fact that this helps you deal with your hazard; however, it likewise opens you up to more chances.

You may likewise get yourself when you have to support your position. Consider a stock position when the outcomes are expected. You may think about taking the contrary position through alternatives, which can help secure your position. When trading movement dies down, you would then be able to loosen up the fence.

As a swing trader, your cash the board system is the one variable that will give you the greatest edge in trading stocks. You can't control the business sectors; however, you can control your cash and your hazard on every single trade that you make.

William O'Neill, the author of Investor's Business Daily, has said that "The entire mystery to winning in the financial exchange is to lose the least sum conceivable when no doubt about it." I would concur with that!

Your cash the executive's procedure addresses these inquiries:

- How a lot of cash would it be a good idea for me to chance on this trade?

- How numerous offers would it be a good idea for me to purchase?

A decent trading framework or system is totally useless without a strategy for dealing with your cash. You like to trade stocks, right? You like to profit in the business sectors, right? Indeed, you won't have any cash to trade with if you don't pursue great cash the executives rehearse!

Your #1 objective as a swing trader is to protect your capital so you can remain alive long enough to have some enormous champs that spread the expenses of your losing trades AND make a benefit. You achieve this through sound cash the board technique.

The 2% rule

Most traders would concur that you ought not to charge over 2% of your trading capital on a solitary trade. The financial exchange is, for the most part, irregular. Nobody else is going to disclose to you this, yet this is the truth of trading stocks.

So regardless of how great the diagram looks, quite possibly the stock won't go in your ideal heading, and you will lose cash on the trade. What amount of cash will you lose if this occurs?

On the first of every month, take a gander at the aggregate sum of cash in your trading account. Suppose you have $30,000. Two percent of this sum is $600.00. That is the greatest sum you can lose on a trade.

Position measuring

Presently suppose that you see a stock that has maneuvered into the TAZ and is currently trading at $25.00. It appears as though it will switch, so you conclude that you are going to trade this stock. You initially need to make sense of where your stop will be. Try not to consider how a lot of cash you can make on a trade; consider how a lot of cash you can lose if your wrong!

I utilize a trade the board programming project called Trade Trakker to monitor my stock trades. Snap here to peruse my survey of this product and view screenshots.

You confirm that your stop will be at $24.00. So, if you purchase the stock at 25.00 and your stop is at $24.00, then your hazard is $1.00 per share. Since you have officially confirmed that the most you can chance on trade are $600.00, then you can purchase 600 portions of this stock.

This is in such a case that you get ceased out you will lose $600.00, the most extreme sum you are permitted to lose. In reality, the number of offers that you purchase ought to be somewhat less because you need to represent slippage and commissions.

By dealing with your cash effectively on each trade, you can unwind in such a case that you bring about misfortune, it will be insignificant to your record. This will likewise assuage the enthusiastic entanglements that plaque such a significant number of traders.

This is just one trade! If you lose cash on this trade, simply proceed onward to another. If you have a string of a few misfortunes in column either quit trading or lessen your position size to 1%.

Cash the board number cruncher

If the majority of this sounds confounding, you might need to get cash the board adding the machine. I got a free one when I purchased the Trading Master Plan.

There are different cash the executive's models to look over. I utilize the Fixed Percent Risk model. On the correct side of the adding machine, you would type in the aggregate sum of cash that you need to trade with. In this model, we are utilizing $20,000. Under that, type in the sum you are eager to hazard per trade. In this model, it is 2%.

Then, on the left side, you type in the value that you are going to purchase the stock at and the cost where your stop misfortune request is going be. For this situation, we are purchasing the stock at $20.00, and our stop misfortune will be at $19.50. Snap ascertain, and it reveals to you precisely what number of offers to purchase: Units to Purchase: 800

This adding machine is a helpful device to have on your work area when you need to rapidly discover what number of offers to purchase. Also, it constrains you to turn into a taught trader by just gambling a little level of your trading capital.

Also, discipline is your key to survival and accomplishment as a swing trader.

TECHNICAL ANALYSIS FOR SWING TRADING

Swing trading consolidates essential and specialized investigation to get groundbreaking value developments while maintaining a strategic distance from inactive occasions. The advantages of this sort of trading area progressively effective utilization of capital and higher returns, and the disadvantages are higher commissions and greater instability.

Swing trading can be difficult for a normal retail trader. The expert traders have more involvement, influence, data, and lower commissions; nonetheless, they are constrained by the instruments they are permitted to trade, the hazard they are fit for taking on and their enormous measure of capital. (Enormous organizations trade in sizes too huge to move all through stocks rapidly.) Knowledgeable retail traders can exploit these things so as to benefit reliably in the commercial center. Here is the thing that a decent day by day swing trading routine and procedure may look like... and you how you can be comparatively fruitful in your trading exercises.

Pre-Market

The retail swing trader will frequently start his day at 6 am EST, a long time before the opening chime. The time

83

before the opening is pivotal for getting a general feel for the day's market, discovering potential trades, making a day by day watch list and, at last, determining the status of existing positions.

The principal undertaking of the day is to make up for lost time with the most recent news and improvements in the business sectors. The fastest method to do this is through the digital TV slot CNBC or legitimate sites, for example, Market Watch. The trader needs to watch out for three things, specifically:

1. Overall market assessment (bullish/bearish, key financial reports, expansion, money, abroad trading sessions, and so on.)

2. Sector assumption (hot areas, developing segments, and so forth.)

3. Current possessions (news, income, SEC filings, and so forth.)

Discover Potential Trades

Next, the trader will check for potential trades for the afternoon. Normally, swing traders will enter a situation with a major impetus and oversee or leave the situation with the guide of specialized investigation. There are two great approaches to discover basic impetuses:

1. Special chances: These are best found by means of SEC filings and, at times, feature news. Such open

doors may incorporate introductory open contributions (IPOs), liquidations, insider purchasing, buyouts, takeovers, mergers, restructurings, acquisitions, and other comparable occasions. Normally, these are found by checking certain SEC filings, for example, S-4 and 13D. This can be effectively finished with the assistance of destinations, for example, SECFilings.com, which will send notifications when such a recording is made. These sorts of chances regularly convey a lot of hazards, yet they convey numerous prizes to the individuals who cautiously look into every chance. These sorts of plays include the swing trader purchasing when most are selling and selling when every other person is purchasing, trying to "blur" eruptions to news and occasions.

2. The sector plays: These are best found by investigating the news or counseling trustworthy money related data sites to discover which areas are performing great. For instance, you can tell that the vitality area is hot basically by checking a well-known vitality trade traded subsidize (like IYE) or examining the news for notices of the vitality division. Traders searching for higher hazard and higher returns may search out increasingly darken segments, for example, coal or titanium. These are frequently a lot harder to investigate, yet they can yield a lot of more prominent returns. These kinds of plays include the swing trader getting tied up

with patterns at advantageous occasions and riding the patterns until there are indications of inversion or retracement.

Diagram breaks are a third sort of chance accessible to swing traders. They are normally intensely traded stocks that are close to a key help or obstruction level. Swing traders will search for a few different sorts of examples intended to foresee breakouts or breakdowns, for example, triangles, channels, Wolfe Waves, Fibonacci levels, Gann levels, and others. Note that diagram breaks are just significant if there is adequate enthusiasm for the stock. These sorts of plays include the swing trader purchasing after a breakout and selling again presently at the following opposition level.

Make a Watch List

The following stage is to make a watch rundown of stocks for the afternoon. These are just stocks that have a principal impetus and a shot at being a decent trade. Some swing traders like to keep a dry-delete board by their trading stations with an ordered rundown of chances, passage costs, target costs, and stop-misfortune costs.

Check Existing Positions

At last, in the pre-showcase hours, the trader must determine the status of their current positions, looking into the news to ensure that nothing material has happened to the stock medium-term. This should be possible by just composing the stock image into a new administration, for example, Google News. Next, traders verify whether any filings have been made via looking through the SEC's EDGAR database. If there is material data, it ought to be investigated to decide if it influences the present trading plan. A trader may likewise need to alter their stop-misfortune, and take-benefit focuses thus.

Market Hours

The market hours are a period of watching and trading. Many swing traders take a gander at level II cites, which will indicate who is purchasing and selling and what sums they are trading. Those originating from the universe of day trading will likewise frequently check which market creator is making the trades (this can prompt traders into who is behind the market producer's trades), and furthermore know about head-counterfeit offers and asks put just to befuddle retail traders.

When a feasible trade has been found and entered, traders start to search for an exit. This is regularly done utilizing specialized examination. Many swing traders like to utilize Fibonacci augmentations, basic obstruction levels or cost by volume. In a perfect world, this is done before the trade has even been put, yet a great deal will regularly rely upon the day's trading. Additionally, alterations may be made later, contingent upon future trading. When in doubt, be that as it may, you ought to never modify a situation to go out on a limb (e.g., move a stop-misfortune down):

possibly alter benefit taking levels if trading keeps on looking bullish, or change stop-misfortune levels upward to secure benefits.

Entering trades is regularly a greater amount of a workmanship than a science, and it will, in general, rely upon the day's trading action. Trade the executives and leaving, then again, ought to dependably be a precise science.

Night-time Market

Night-time trading is once in a while utilized as an opportunity to place trades because the market is illiquid and the spread is frequently an excessive amount to justify. The most significant part of twilight trading is execution assessment. It is imperative to painstakingly record all trades and thoughts for both assessment purposes and execution assessment. Execution assessment includes investigating all trading action and identifying things that need improvement. At long last, a trader should audit their open positions one final time, giving specific consideration to twilight profit declarations, or other material occasions that may affect the property.

Candles and oscillators can be utilized freely, or in the mix, to feature potential transient trading openings. Swing traders have practical experience in utilizing specialized examination to exploit momentary value moves. Effectively trading these swings requires the capacity to precisely decide both patterns bearing and pattern quality. This should be possible using graph designs, oscillators, volume investigation, fractals, and an assortment of different techniques. This article will concentrate on utilizing oscillators and candle examples to identify swing trades.

Pinpointing a Reversal

Swing traders can search for momentary inversions in the cost to catch pending value moves toward that path. The initial step is to locate the correct conditions for an inversion, which should be possible with either candles or oscillators. Candle inversions are portrayed by hesitation candles or candles that demonstrate a solid shift in opinion (from purchasing to selling or offering to purchasing), while oscillator feature potential inversions through uniqueness.

Oscillator Divergence

Uniqueness is when the cost is moving the other way of a forced oscillator. Consider it in material science terms: if you toss a ball open to question, it loses energy before it inverts heading. This is likewise how inversions can happen in the securities exchange. Force moderates before stock costs switch. Dissimilarity may indicate when the force is abating, and a potential inversion is inevitable. Not all value inversions are conjecture by difference, however many are.

The disparity is a decent beginning stage for a trade. The difference doesn't generally need to show, however, if dissimilarity is available, the candle designs (examined straightaway) are probably going to be all the more dominant and prone to result in better trades.

The accompanying outline indicates disparity. The cost was moving higher; however, the oscillator—the relative quality list (RSI), for this situation—was moving lower. The difference demonstrated shortcoming in the ascent, which was additionally obvious by taking a gander at the value activity as the cost could scarcely make new highers before falling once more. Eventually, the value wound up falling significantly.

The subsequent stage is to characterize a careful (or as close as could be allowed) purpose of inversion. This assignment is best cultivated utilizing specific candle designs. Even though there are more than 50 different candle designs, here we will concentrate on two of the more typical ones.

Bullish and Bearish Engulfing Patterns

Bullish and bearish immersing examples are probably the most mainstream candle designs. An overwhelming bearish example is portrayed by the cost moving higher, ordinarily appeared green or white candles. Then there is an enormous downlight, regularly hued red or dark, which is bigger than the latest up to the flame. The downlight totally wraps the earlier up flame, appearing solid selling has entered the market. Trades are taken close to the end of the bearish inundating flame, or close to the accompanying open.

An overwhelming bullish example is an inverse. The cost is falling, and afterward, there is an enormous up light that encompasses the earlier down flame, demonstrating purchasers have entered the market forcefully.

Hesitation Candles

The turning top example is another normal candle inversion design. It is a little body with long tails. It indicates uncertainty on the grounds that there is instability all through the period; however, before the finish of the period, the cost is close where it began. While turning tops may happen on their claim and sign a pattern change, a few will regularly happen together. The cost will then make a significant move one way or the other, and close toward that path. That is the heading to trade in.

CANDLESTICK ANALYSIS AND CHART PATTERNS FOR SWING TRADING

Swing Trading a moderately prevalent trading system. The coming of PCs in the course of the last seven to ten years has opened the open door for speculators to trade stocks and different ventures from their home or office. The huge improvement in graphing administrations on the Internet currently gives a technique to people to exploit the brisk vacillations in stock costs. Swing trading gives speculators a colossal chance to make benefits.

As the market assessments advance, long haul contributing turns out to be, to a lesser degree a prevailing type of contributing. Swing trading has numerous points of interest over long haul contributing, particularly when executing with a planning procedure, for example, candle trading. Swing Traders will regularly hold a specific stock for anyplace from a couple of days to half a month yet trade based on the stock's intra-week or intra-month value changes.

Candle investigation has "the presence of mind" incorporated with its sign. Understanding the financial specialist assumption readies the candle speculator to augment benefits in momentary swing trading. To get into a trade at the ideal point, envisioning when a pattern is going to switch, is critical. Seeing how the normal financial specialist thinks and responds allows quick benefits to be made by swing trading.

When most patterns turn around, they do as such with life. The underlying day or two of a pattern inversion can deliver magnificent benefits. Swing trading is focused after exploiting that underlying move. If the trader has the instruments to discover and misuse these moves, swing trading turns into a productive and agreeable type of extricating benefits from the market. Our conflict is that the candle sign ARE the devices required.

Swing trading requires the arrangement and convergence of occasions to augment benefits. Long haul contributing does not require the stringent examination of benefit parameters. How regularly have you heard someone defend about misfortune in their position, "Gracious well, I'm in it as long as possible." This announcement is frequently articulated as opposed to taking a dynamic position towards one's venture objectives.

Swing trading speaks to the precise inverse. A financial specialist attempting to amplify benefits from a two to multi-day holding period must have investigated all components. When swing trading, the foundation of trade must correct in its motivation, making a benefit NOW in that trade.

The intrinsic attributes incorporated with candle sign produce the parameters that make swing trading effective. The acknowledgment of example inversion in a pattern can be outwardly delineated in the sign. For the forceful swing trader, knowing how the sign is framed can deliver trades that pinpoint the accurate point where to enter a trade. Also, similar signs that get the candle swing trader into a trade will alarm the trader when the time has come to get out.

As found in the accompanying outline, see the Doji signals at each turn. Realizing what to do after each sign makes the configuration for beneficial swing trading. Knowing the straightforward guidelines about what to do once watching a Doji has the candle swing trader all through trades at the ideal focuses.

Learning the techniques to assess the sign makes swing trading a simple program to concentrate benefits out of the market reliably. Candle sign gives two important aspects. To start with, the sign ventures find the high potential productive swing trades. The pursuits can be developed to discover the sign that happens at the best positions during pattern development. Finding a candle purchase signal when stochastics are oversold or scanning for a hole up after a Doji are a few models on the most proficient method to completely use the pursuit capacities. The subsequent aspect is the pinpointing when to get into and out of a trade as clarified before.

Candle diagrams are a specialized apparatus that pack information for various time spans into single value bars. This makes them more helpful than customary open-high, low-close bars (OHLC) or basic lines that come to an obvious conclusion of shutting costs. Candles assemble designs that anticipate value heading once finished. Appropriate shading coding adds profundity to this vivid specialized instrument, which goes back to eighteenth-century Japanese rice traders.

Steve Nison brought candle examples toward the Western world in his famous 1991 book, "Japanese Candlestick Charting Techniques." Many traders would now be able to identify many these arrangements, which have beautiful names like bearish foreboding shadow spread, evening star and three dark crows. Furthermore, single bar examples, including the doji and sled have been fused into many long-and short-side trading systems.

Candle Pattern Reliability

Not all candle examples work similarly well. Their immense notoriety has brought down dependability since they've been deconstructed by speculative stock investments and their calculations. These well-subsidized players depend on lightning-speed execution to trade against retail speculators and customary reserve supervisors who execute specialized investigation procedures found in prevalent writings. At the end of the day, support investments managers use programming to trap members searching for high-chances bullish or bearish results. In any case, solid examples keep on showing up, taking into account short and long-haul benefit openings.

Here are five candle designs that perform incredibly well as forerunners of value-bearing and energy. Every work inside the setting of encompassing value bars in anticipating higher or lower costs. They are additionally time delicate in two different ways. In the first place, they just work inside the restrictions of the graph being checked on, regardless of whether intraday, every day, week after week or month to month. Second, their intensity diminishes quickly three to five bars after the example has finished.

Top 5 Candlestick Patterns

This investigation depends on crafted by Thomas Bulkowski, who manufactured execution rankings for candle designs in his 2008 book, "Reference book of Candlestick Charts." He offers insights for two sorts of expected example results: reversal and continuation. Candle inversion examples anticipate an adjustment in value bearing, while continuation examples foresee an augmentation in the present value heading.

In the accompanying models, the empty white candle signifies an end print higher than the opening print, while the dark candle means an end print lower than the opening print.

Three Line Strike

The bullish three-line strike inversion example cuts out three dark candles inside a downtrend. Each bar posts a lower low and closes close to the intrabar low. The fourth bar opens even lower yet inverts in a wide-run outside bar that closes over the high of the main light in the arrangement. The opening print additionally denotes the low of the fourth bar. As indicated by Bulkowski, this inversion predicts more expensive rates with an 84% precision rate.

Two Black Gapping

The bearish two dark gapping continuation example shows up after a remarkable top in an upturn, with a hole down that yields two dark bars posting lower lows. This example predicts that the decrease will keep on night lower lows, maybe setting off a more extensive scale downtrend. As indicated by Bulkowski, this example predicts lower costs with a 68% exactness rate.

Three Black Crows

The bearish three dark crows inversion example begins at or close to the high of an upturn, with three dark bars posting lower lows that nearby, close intrabar lows. This example predicts that the decay will keep on night lower lows, maybe setting off a more extensive scale downtrend. The most bearish rendition begins at another high (point an on the graph) since it traps purchasers entering force plays.

As indicated by Bulkowski, this example predicts lower costs with a 78% exactness rate.

Night Star

The bearish night star inversion example begins with a tall white bar that conveys an upswing to another high. The market holes higher on the following bar, yet new purchasers neglect to show up, yielding a restricted range candle. A hole down on the third bar finishes the example, which predicts that the decrease will keep on night lower lows, maybe setting off a more extensive scale downtrend. As indicated by Bulkowski, this example predicts lower costs with a 72% precision rate.

Relinquished Baby

The bullish relinquished child inversion example shows up at the low of a downtrend after a progression of dark candles prints lower lows. The market holes lower on the following bar, however, crisp vendors neglect to show up, yielding a thin range Doji candle with opening and shutting prints at a similar cost. A bullish hole on the third bar finishes the example, which predicts that the recuperation will keep on night higher highs, maybe setting off a more extensive scale upturn. As indicated by Bulkowski, this example predicts more expensive rates with a 70% exactness rate.

SWING TRADING WITH TOOLS AND INDICATORS

This is a speedy review of three of the best trading pointers for day and swing traders alike. If you are another trader, then it is significant for you to comprehend that no marker or oscillator is going to make you trade beneficially promptly, so don't go on a pointless pursuit to discover one that will. Get familiar with a chosen few pointers and the techniques and methodologies to utilize them successfully. Ace them, and after that, find out additional.

"Your system will be increasingly gainful, utilizing fewer pointers that you have aced. Then more markers that you haven't."

How about we start.

Moving Averages (MA)

Moving Averages put essentially are simply lines that are determined by past costs. They are straightforward and are incredibly valuable with any trading sort, regardless of whether that is an intraday, swing, or considerably longer trading styles.

You ought to dependably have various MA lines with differentiating timeframes on your graph. I, for one, utilize three MAs: multi-day MA, multi-day MA, and a multi-day MA. This gives me a more extensive perspective available and helps me identify more grounded patterns and inversions.

WAYS TO USE MOVING AVERAGES

1.) Identifying Trend Strength

Put basically, the more remote away the present cost and pattern are from its relative moving normal, the more fragile that pattern is, helping you the trader, spot potential inversions and discovering passages and ways out. This technique in great practice is utilized related to different markers like volume. (underneath).

2.) Identifying Trend Reversals with Crossovers

For the most part, MA hybrids can be signals for pattern inversions, for instance, if the nine-day MA crosses underneath the multi-day MA after an upswing. Then the bullish pattern might turn around flagging a bearish pattern. Be cautioned, however, because there will, in general, be incessant phony outs with hybrids that find new traders napping; you ought to dependably make a point to affirm inversions utilizing different techniques and instruments.

Moving Averages are significant because they give traders a comprehension of the business sectors states, never trade aimlessly.

Relative Strength Index (RSI)

The RSI marker gives a general assessment of the quality of a security's present value, utilizing it's past exhibition and instability. Once more, this is another must-have for a trader and additionally trading style.

The RSI scores security on a size of 1–100, you should recollect this for the tips beneath.

RSI Can be Used a Number of Ways

1.) Identifying Overbought/Oversold Conditions

Identifying overbought/oversold conditions is helpful in discovering pattern inversions or adjustments. When security is overbought, it can flag a bearish pattern inversion or a rectification; when a security is oversold, it can flag a bullish pattern inversion or adjustment.

The course reading numbers for these conditions is 70/30: 70 = overbought/exaggerated, 30 oversold / underestimated. In spite of the fact that with an end goal to lessen phony outs, a few traders (counting me) use 80/20 for those conditions.

2.) Identifying Divergences

Traders can likewise utilize divergences to identify pattern inversions; a dissimilarity is a difference or contradiction (connection to Merriam Webster beneath).

Bullish Divergent Signal

When the value makes a new low, yet the RSI does not (or proportional).

Bearish Divergent Signal

When the value makes another high however the RSI does not (or comparable)

Snappy huge developments will make counterfeit outs (false flag). So simply like some other marker, dependably affirm patterns with different instruments/strategies.

Volume

Utilizing Volume in trading is extremely straightforward; however, it is normally neglected by new traders. Clearly, it is significant for good liquidity... yet the standard that truly changed how I traded when I was learning was this.

"Patterns should be upheld by volume, dependable guarantee heavier volume is occurring toward a pattern."

Learning this improved my game generously. When an upturn in cost is in play, new cash should bolster it, so you have to see the rising volume. The other way around with downtrends. If this isn't going on, then this is an indication of exaggerated or underestimated conditions.

Most financial specialists will purchase their positions and after that clutch them, sitting tight for economic situations to improve before they make a trade. Along these lines, they can profit by a decent return. There are those financial specialists who are unimaginably understanding, sitting tight for quite a long time and gathering little profits after some time as their profits. Then there are those that are in a rush to get their profits, particularly if there is a little gratefulness in the pair they are trading. That is the thing that swings trading is about. To benefit as much as possible from this procedure, you have to realize these three swing trading markers.

1. Moving Average

The first is the moving normal where the emphasis is on identifying a pattern as well as affirming the pattern. The most straightforward moving normal pointer to utilize is the basic moving normal. It necessitates that all the shutting costs be included down for a specific number of days, and after that, taking the aggregate and separating it by a similar number. On a diagram, it is conceivable to plot the normal so one can comprehend what's going on with the market cost.

2. Relative Strength Index

To decide the best positions in the swing market for swing trading, you additionally look over the second pointer, which is among the best-specialized markers for swing trading. This is the RSI which represents the Relative Strength Index. This marker gives data that is perfect to section into the market. It assists with the examination of a short flag, under a specific assumption. That is the reality the market might be overbought or might be oversold. It is an astounding procedure when the market has demonstrated to be level just as range bound.

3. Visual Analysis Indicator

Specialized markers give an abundance of data, however here and there, it is a lot simpler to have a visual example of working with. This makes it a lot simpler to perceive what's going on inside the market and guide your choice. This is the third swing trading marker, visual investigation. There are a few examples that one can pay special mind to particularly as a pointer for a swing trading system.

TIPS TO MAKE YOU A BETTER SWING TRADER

Since you know the best swing trade pointers, here are a few hints that will make you a brilliant swing trader. Begin off by identifying your help just as opposition levels utilizing specialized examination. This implies you ought to have the option to peruse the diagram to decide the territory inside the graph where there is some help or opposition.

Figure out how to identify wide range of candles as these make it simpler to uncover defining moments inside the swing trade. With this, you will almost certainly discover when a stock may turn around.

Swing trading is the key to progress for some traders. Investigate it, contemplate how it is done, and make fast profits for abrupt changes in the market.

WHY YOU SHOULD BEGIN WITH SWING TRADING

You chose to make a stride that 46% of Americans don't take; putting resources into the securities exchange. It tends to be terrifying to consider. Losing cash unnerves many individuals, naturally.

The truth is that putting resources into the financial exchange should be possible securely if you make the correct strides.

That is the thing that Trader Lab is about.

So, where do you begin?

What stocks would it be advisable for you to put resources into?

What amount would it be advisable for me to put into each stock?

First of all, you need an online dealer, which is what we will talk about here.

If you plan on long haul contributing and not trading, then you ought to consider opening up a Robinhood account. You can purchase and sell stocks sans commission, which means more cash for you to contribute.

If you plan on purchasing and selling a similar stock inside multi day's time (multi-day trade), then you need at any rate $25,000 in your record. If you don't have $25,000 to trade, then you would probably need to figure out how to swing trade (purchasing a selling inside a 2-to-multi-day timespan). We center around swing trading at Trader Lab as we probably are aware most understudies or even school graduates don't have $25,000 to trade with.

If you plan on day trading, you might need to consider E* Trade or TD Ameritrade for your online merchant. These all charge an expense for purchasing and selling your stock, which cut into your benefits, yet their stages seemingly have significantly more to offer than Robinhood.

If you plan on swing trading, you can browse almost any confided in representative as the Pattern Day Trader (PDT) guideline would not concern you since you would hold stocks medium-term.

WHAT STOCKS TO SWING TRADE?

One of the principal things you will gain from preparing recordings, webcasts, and client aides is that you have to pick the correct protections. As far as stocks, for instance, the huge top stocks frequently have the degrees of volume and instability you need. These stocks will ordinarily swing between higher highs and genuine lows. This implies you can swing one way for a couple of days and afterward, when you spot inversion designs, you can swap to the contrary side of the trade.

Finding the correct stock picks is one of the rudiments of a swing technique. A valuable tip to push you to that end is to pick a stage with compelling screeners and scanners. There's essentially no utilization having the best methodology if you're estimating on the off-base low-evaluated stocks.

The Right Market

Swing trading can be especially testing in the two market limits, the bear showcase condition or seething buyer advertise. Here you will discover even profoundly dynamic stocks won't show the equivalent here and their motions as when files are fairly steady for a considerable length of time.

Rather, you will discover in a bear or positively trending business sector that energy will typically convey stocks for a significant period in a solitary course. This can affirm the best passage point and technique is based on the more extended term pattern.

Basically then, it is when the business sectors aren't going anyplace that you have the perfect swing trading condition. For instance, if you were to trade on the Nasdaq, you would need the file to ascend for two or three days, decrease for a few days and after that recurrent the example. So albeit following a couple of months your stock might associate with introductory levels, you have had various chances to gain by transient vacillations.

Utilizing the Exponential Moving Average

A swing trading institute will run you through alarms, holes, rotate focuses, and specialized markers. However, maybe one of the fundamental standards they will walk you through is the exponential moving normal (EMA).

This is basically a variety of the straightforward moving normal yet with an expanded spotlight on the most recent information focuses. Utilized effectively it can enable you to identify pattern flag just as section and leave focuses a lot quicker than a basic moving normal can. Basically, you can utilize the EMA hybrid to assemble your entrance and leave methodology.

Application

An EMA framework is clear and can include in swing trading methodologies for amateurs. You can utilize the nine-, 13-and 50-period EMAs. Your bullish hybrid will show up at the point the value breaks over the moving midpoints subsequent to beginning beneath.

This reveals to you an inversion and an upswing might be going to become possibly the most important factor. Then if your nine-period EMA surpasses the 13-time frame EMA, this alarms you to a long section. Having said that, the 13-time frame EMA must be over the 50-time frame EMA or really cross above it.

On the other side, a bearish hybrid happens if the cost of an advantage falls underneath the EMAs. This lets you know there could be a potential inversion of a pattern. You would then be able to utilize this to time your exit from a long position.

So, if the nine-time frame EMA breaks the 13-time frame EMA, this alarms you to a short passage or the need to leave a long position. Having said that, the 13-time frame EMA must be beneath the 50-time frame EMA or cross underneath.

Use the EMA accurately, with the opportune time spans and the correct security in your line of sight, and you have every one of the basics of a successful swing system.

THE BRAIN SCIENCE OF SWING TRADING

It is genuine you can download an entire host of digital broadcasts, book recordings, and PDFs that will give you instances of swing trading, standards to pursue and Heiken-Ashi diagrams to fabricate. Be that as it may, what they regularly won't let you know is how to rationally respond when your swing trading technique doesn't work.

So, you ought to think about the accompanying three hints:

1. Have an arrangement and stick to it – There will be highs and lows, that is the very idea of purchasing and selling in the business sectors. In any case, let the maths manage those high points and low points, don't give your feelings a chance to act as a burden. Choosing when to sell can rapidly turn into a passionate choice when you have your entire weeks returns on hold. Along these lines, detail a methodology and after that stick to it religiously.

2. Combat dread by lessening hazard – Everyone's craving for hazard is different. So, discover chance parameters that suit. For instance, you might need to begin by not gambling over 2% of your record estimate on a solitary trade. This is something no tutor can educate you. Just through long periods of

training will you realize where your own breaking points are.

3. Think long haul – Too numerous traders fixates on the last trade or the following. Try not to stress if you simply lost on gold prospects. Rather, consider your long-haul benefit rate and adding machine. As Bruce Kovner suitably called attention to, "If you customize misfortunes, you can't trade."

Swing Trading Top Tips

Indeed, even probably the best swing books forget a portion of the top tips and insider facts of swing trading, including:

- Utilize the news – Markets are always moving in response to news occasions. Numerous assets, for example, Yahoo Finance and CNBC, will give advertise examination and discourse, utilizing volume, value activity, and week by week graphs. In this way, utilized accurately, the news could enable you to feature potential alternatives and profit stocks to watch out for, for instance. It could likewise enable you to design your entrances and exits.

- Never quit learning – As Paul Tudor Jones broadly stated: "The key to being fruitful from a trading point of view is to have an inexhaustible and an undying and voracious hunger for data and information." There is an abundance of data accessible to support you create powerful digital currency and swing methodologies. Video instructional exercises, for instance, can help show you Gann systems and how to begin utilizing week after week somewhere down in the cash alternatives. They can likewise run you through markers for your MT4 stage and the setting up of everyday stock alarms.

- Find the correct dealer and trade – Everyone has different needs and needs, so while one crypto swing trader might be best off on Gdax or Binance, an exceptionally dynamic swing trader might need to consider Dailyfx. Note they are likewise in excess of a spot to consider statements and trade protections. They can enable you to fabricate a differing watchlist, portfolio, thus substantially more.

- Keep a Journal – Keeping an Excel diary can demonstrate pricelessly. Basically, note down value, date, position measure, and an explanation behind the section and leave focuses. This could enable you to perceive any reason why your breakouts plan for cash sets does not take a shot at week after week graphs, for instance

The amount of Money Can You Make?

Swing trading profits depend altogether for the trader. For instance, take utilized ETFs versus stocks, some will yield liberal comes back with the previous while flopping hopelessly with the last mentioned, regardless of the two trades being moderately comparable.

It will likewise halfway rely upon the methodology you take. A few people will adulate MACD pointers while others use an NMA framework. Much the same as some will swear by utilizing candle graphing with help and obstruction levels, while some will trade on the news.

The key is to discover a methodology that works for you and around your timetable. See our techniques page to have the subtleties of defining a trading plan clarified.

#1 Money

To this point, I need to dig into the theme of the stuff to swing trade professionally, as this could be another road for our perusers to seek after profiting in the business sectors.

Swing trading is a different creature than day trading, as you can't follow if you have won or misfortune on a given day.

In this book, I will cover the 5 things required to effcctively swing trade professionally, which will help beat the difficulties of not having the option to intently track and screen your trading execution.

How about we begin by examining the conspicuous thing required for fruitful swing trading - cash. Dissimilar to day trading where you can use up to multiple times your money, swing trading will expect you to hold positions medium-term, so you won't most likely dive in. Best case scenario, you could hold double the size of your money account by utilizing edge. In any case, I wouldn't prescribe going out on a limb on that degree of hazard as you are trading professionally.

Single and No Kids

To stroll through the required supports expected to swing trade professionally, we are going to initially accept our anecdotal trader is single without any children.

I cherish my children, yet the genuine multifaceted nature of life kicks in once you are in charge of another person. You need to begin considering things like attire, nourishment, extracurricular exercises, and school reserve funds. Easily, the costs simply start to include up you.

When you are single without children, you don't have any of these stresses. Your solitary concern is to deal with yourself, so you will have more squirm stay with the expectations for everyday comforts your expectations for everyday comforts.

For this situation, we should accept you have $3,500 in complete everyday costs every month. Over the course of a year, this signifies $42,000. Since we are burdened so intensely here in the States, this would liken to a gross trading pay of around $55,000 every year just to make back the initial investment.

Since we have our number, we should again into the base measure of money we would require in our trading record to endure.

If we have a beginning record of $100,000 and expecting we were just going to utilize money, we would need to make a normal of 4.2% every month. This sounds entirely sensible superficially, yet a couple of things fly in my brain.

To begin with, its quite difficult to make a steady 4.2% every month with the majority of the outer market factors out of your control, which are constantly present when trading.

Also, you can't develop the record, since you have to pull back each dime you make in the market. Presently, if you have an all-day work, taking all of the money out would be a non-issue; be that as it may, swing trading is your lone wellspring of pay.

Plainly, the number should be somewhat higher to make them inhale room. For contentions purpose, I would state to successfully swing trade; you need around multiple times your month to month costs.

Did you simply drop out of your seat? I know there will be individuals that perused this that figure they can bring home the bacon on $50,000. Very much given me a chance to squash the commotion as the chances are solidly against you.

If you have $350,000, you could actually go a whole year without making a dime in trading and still be in the game. This is what it's about. The capacity to remain in the game.

Sole Breadwinner

We should go to the next outrageous for discourse purposes and spread an imaginary nuclear family with a sole provider. How about we accept all out month to month costs run you about $10k.

If you fall into this basin, you would require an incredible $1M dollars outside of your investment funds to swing trade professionally.

The truth is out an entire 1 Million dollars. As I expressed previously, you can generally begin with less cash; be that as it may, less cash approaches more pressure and more noteworthy trading dangers. Everything comes down to the personal satisfaction you are hoping to accommodate your family.

As should be obvious, the degree of cash expected obviously increase significantly the more individuals you have in your family unit.

If you are single, you shouldn't utilize this as motivation to put your life on hold until you achieve specific record esteem, since you would prefer not to be secured. The exact opposite thing you ought to ever do is put your life on hold looking out for the market to come through.

You simply need to design in like manner. One thing you could do to reduce the hazard is if you and your mate both works. Along these lines, you can have medical coverage and the subsequent pay coming into the family unit. This would normally diminish the measure of beginning capital required on your end.

There are huge amounts of other inventive things you can do to accomplish your fantasy of swing trading professionally; you simply need to thoroughly consider them all and recall that some advancement is great.

#2 - Time Box Your Trades

An extraordinary aspect regarding day trading is that you're restricted continuously, the market is open. Well, welcome to the universe of swing trading, where things aren't so plainly characterized.

To more readily characterize the limits inside which you live, you have to set a period limit on to what extent you will remain in a position. Presently, there will be those of you that will say, let your champs run.

Well yes and no. If you have to pay your home loan, the main way I realize how to do that is to remove money from the market. You can't compose your home loan organization an IOU solicitation dependent on your paper benefits.

This carries me to my point; you have to adjust the time required to finish a swing, with the misfortune chance of sitting in a level position. To this point, the greatest time allotment I would hold a situation for swing trading is 4 a month and a half.

Reason being, swing trading is tied in with getting the following swing, so your capital is inconsistent movement and not secured sitting tight for the grand slam trade or the multi-year venture. If you continue settling on sound trading choices, you will be on a consistent up direction and not giving your cash a chance to lounge around for a considerable length of time doing nothing.

Subsequently, I don't get this' meaning for your primary concern? You will require enough money to guarantee you can cover your costs while you are hanging tight to finish off your trade, as things could without much of a stretch go past the 30-day cycle of our everyday costs.

Try not to peruse this to be more than what it is. Dislike the majority of your yearly bills will have an inflatable installment, it's simply you should be set up to have some money saves accessible and not all tied up in the market in the occasion you have to pay your bills.

Ultimately, time boxing your trades will compel you to reliably remove cash from the market, so the money is genuine to you and not pixels on a screen. Taking cash out will likewise support you and your life partner or significant other understand that what you are doing is not kidding and not a side interest as they see the positive effects trading is having on your nuclear family.

#3 - Diversification

If you lose track of what's most important while day trading and over influence a position, you can at present oversee through the trade. Notwithstanding, if you concentrate your swing trade position, you could lose a significant part of your assets if things go the incorrect way medium-term.

In this way, to alleviate the hazard, you have to diversify your property. The test you will face is that you have to limit your dangers; in any case, you have to have the option to turn a better than average enough benefit and utmost the number of trades you have to oversee.

In principle, I would state go with minimal measure of positions, while having the option to limit your dangers. In light of this prerequisite, the correct number of trades to convey in the meantime would be somewhere close to 3 and 4. This gives you enough position fixation that you can make a tolerable profit for your speculation, yet at the same time have room schedule-wise and center to successfully deal with each position.

If you end up supposing, "I should hold 10 positions to further decrease my hazard", then you have an absence of faith in your framework and aren't prepared to begin swing trading professionally. You are likely most appropriate for long haul contributing where you are eager to hold positions over an all-encompassing timeframe.

Give me a chance to help give you a visual of what overseeing just 6 positions would resemble to help commute home this point.

Presently suppose you add an extra 10 to this rundown. You would be required to continually screen these positions both during and outside of market hours.

While there is a view of less hazard, there are different negatives, which enormously lessen the viability of this degree of diversification.

#4 - Winning System

In this way, this is basically an easy decision. Regardless of the amount you plan or how a lot of money you have available, you need to succeed at trading the business sectors. This comes down to the nature of your trading framework and your capacity to reliably turn a benefit.

Anyway, what does a triumphant framework intend to you? For me, there is just a single thing, reliable benefits. I would mind less if I have a greater number of victors than washouts, if by the day's end I'm not turning a benefit, it implies literally nothing.

#5 - Winning Attitude

If you approach the business sectors with your shoulders hanging and little confidence, you will lose after some time. What you escape the market is an immediate impression of your association with cash and your own view of self-esteem.

If you are tight with your assets, you will be tight with your stops. If you don't esteem the cash in your record, then you will figure out how to blow it.

When you are home trading, or in a little office, nobody will be there to help push you through a difficult time. You should burrow profound to discover the fortitude and they would like to see through the intense occasions.

WHY SWING TRADING GIVES YOU THE BEST CHANCE TO SUCCEED

If trading appears to be disappointing and difficult to you, don't stress, you are not the only one. Numerous traders, if not most, start their trading vocations with grandiose objectives and a full tank of expectation, yet those things can blur all around rapidly if you aren't moving toward the market from the right 'point.'

At Learn to Trade the Market, we take the view that whether a retail trader (like you or I) makes steady progress in the market depends intensely on which strategy the trader employments. In other words, we accept if you are trading with the off-base procedure, it is highly unlikely you will ever profit, regardless of whether you're doing everything else right.

Trading achievement is the final product of getting the "3 M's" correct; Method, Mindset, and Money Management. You can't prevail with just two of the three; you should have each of the three under control.

In this exercise, I need to concentrate on the principal M; the Method that will give you the most obvious opportunity to prevail at trading. You have to comprehend which strategy is the best, why it is the best and how you can ace it, so how about we begin…

Swing Trading: The retail trader's just genuine shot

I won't deceive you; as a retail Swing trader, or a retail trader of any market truly, there are different 'powers' neutralizing you, which you may or not have known about as of not long ago. Frankly, with you, you are a one-man (or lady) group when you're a trader, and except if you approach incredibly enormous entireties of cash/the capacity to withstand huge drawdowns, you are not going to keep going longer if you don't utilize the best possible trading strategy.

The huge players in the market, similar to banks, speculative stock investments, and so forth know where littler retail traders put in their requests and what they normally 'do' in the market (purchase breakouts, day-trade, and so forth.). They know all the little clock methodologies, and in all honesty, they appreciate taking your cash each day in the market. You can't make due without a stop misfortune; however they can, or if nothing else, they can for longer stretch than you or I and this is the reason day trading is risky; on the grounds that traders put exceptionally little/tight stop misfortunes on their positions they frequently get halted out by typical everyday value vacillations in the market.

I'm not going to state that your representative 'needs you to lose,' however, I think saying they need you to day-trade is a reasonable appraisal. For what reason do they need you to day-trade you inquire? Indeed, for the one, you will produce a lot of charges as spread installments or commissions, and two, you will lose a ton of trades for the reason I talked about in the past passage. So, day-trading is a trick's down that sucks individuals in by engaging their eager/fretful want to make 'quick cash.'

On the furthest edge of the trading scale, we have position trading or contributing, this is fundamentally long haul purchase and hold procedures that while they may satisfy when you are prepared to resign, they are not reasonable for anybody hoping to bring home the bacon as a trader, similar to you and I.

That carries us to what I call the trading 'sweet spot'; swing trading. If you don't definitely know, this is what swing trading is: Swing Trading is a strategy for specialized examination to enable you to spot solid directional moves in the market that keep going overall, two to six days. Swing trading permits singular traders like us to misuse the solid transient moves made by huge institutional traders who can't move all through the market as fast.

What is a 'swing point' in the market?

To place this in a little less complex terms, I'm expecting you have taken a gander at a fundamental value diagram previously. If you have, you likely see that business sectors don't move in straight lines for exceptionally long. Rather, the cost will 'swing' from high to depressed spots in the market. Particularly in a drifting business sector, these graph swing focuses are basic focuses on a value diagram where we can envision a value activity sign to frame at, and that frequently give high-likelihood passages just before a pattern is preparing to continue.

The diagram underneath demonstrates to us what swing high focuses and swing depressed spots resemble. This market was slanting higher, so as to swing traders, we would have searched for a section close to the swing lows...

Swing trading is the craftsmanship and ability to peruse a value diagram to foresee the following 'swing' in the market. I use value activity trading methodologies to discover high-likelihood sections in the market at these swing focuses; you may see me allude to this as 'purchasing shortcoming's or 'purchasing the dunks' in a rising business sector and 'selling quality' or 'selling the revives' in a falling business sector. This wording alludes to the general methodology that a swing trader utilizes; purchasing as a market tumbles down and ideally purchasing the swing depressed spot (or near it) inside an up-inclining market, the inverse would be the situation for a down pattern obviously.

Different reasons why you ought to turn into a swing trader

Since we've talked about what swing trading is and the primary motivation behind why you have to learn it and make it your trading strategy, we should examine a portion of different advantages of it.

Day by day outlines

As I've expounded on finally in different articles; when you trade the day by day outline time span as a swing trader does, you are receiving numerous rewards contrasted with those poor spirits who still think scalping a 5-minute diagram is the way to progress.

One reason why swing trading is such an immense bit of leeway to the retail trader is that it enables you to avoid all the market 'commotion' of brief time spans, similar to those under the 1-hour outline. Merchants and the huge institutional traders WANT littler retail traders to trade brief time allotments and day-trade/scalp since they realize they will get your cash effectively if you do.

Swing trading on higher time allotments like the 4 hour and day by day enables you to piggyback off the enormous moves made by the greater players in the market, and it likewise enables you to put your stop misfortune outside of their achieve, subsequently giving you more noteworthy 'resilience' with the goal that you can remain in the market longer and increment your odds of getting on board a major, gainful move.

Fit trading in around your calendar

Swing trading enables you to fit trading in around whatever bustling calendar you may have, or if you don't have a bustling timetable, it will enable you to make cash trading and still make the most of your spare time. There's nothing more exhausting than sitting before the diagrams throughout the day, also that it's terrible for your trading and your wellbeing.

Swing trading enables you to examine the business sectors on your calendar, for brief timeframes, in light of the fact that you are concentrating on higher time spans as referenced previously. Additionally, in light of the fact that you are holding your trades for multi-day or more, as a rule, you can enter a trade on a Tuesday suppose, then rest and get up multi-day later and mind your trade. You don't have to stay there throughout the night stressing over your trades, nor should you. A nearly 'supernatural' thing happens when you quit giving such a great amount of consideration to your trades; you begin to see better trading outcomes.

Individuals over-muddle their trading by basically being excessively included. Swing trading is the best strategy since it's correlative to how you ought to act in the market since it rewards you for being less included and taking fewer trades after some time, which is actually what you have to would if you like to get an opportunity at progress. The bring home message here is, swing trading will enable you to maintain a strategic distance from over-trading, and over-trading is the most compelling motivation why individuals lose their cash trading.

SWING TRADING STRATEGIES FOR BEGINNERS AND FOR ADVANCED

If you were to take a swing trading course at the present time, I accept that the present economic situations would permit any trader utilizing the correct trading system to convey strong outcomes. There are a couple of things that I figure we ought to consider before beginning.

One of those is to decide whether we should trade a counter pattern framework or a drifting stock arrangement. It is possible that one can work, yet it is dependent upon you to figure out which one you need to utilize. I suggest utilizing paper trading on a stock swing whenever you see one create.

This article will go top to bottom about a key swing trading strategy on day by day graphs. While this might be viewed as cutting edge swing trading, this technique is appropriate for all speculators. It is ideal for home investigation. We will disclose to you how to do a legitimate specialized examination and demonstrate to you when to enter the trade and when to leave the trade. We will do this by showing you how to set the correct benefit target.

It is critical to ensure you have a completely created preparing plan before beginning to trade any swing trading framework. This will enable you to get ready to turn out to be increasingly fruitful and join the positions of expert informal investors. It is our objective to give you the trading openings, just as to assistance you inside and out that we can to turn into the best swing traders around. You can likewise get familiar with how investors trade in the swing market.

Swing trading methodologies are truly straightforward. Utilizing a middle of the road time allotment (ordinarily a couple of days to half a month), swing traders will identify market patterns and open positions. The name swing trading originates from the way that we are searching at conditions where costs are probably going to swing either upwards or downwards.

Swing traders can utilize a wide exhibit of specialized pointers. What makes swing trading remarkable is that it mixes a few parts of day trading, with the speed of position trading. Swing trading markers are basically used to discover patterns that happen somewhere in the range of 3 and 15 trading periods. After we break down these periods, we will most likely decide if cases of opposition or backing have happened.

The subsequent stage is to identify the bearish or bullish pattern and search for inversions. Inversions are frequently alluded to as pullbacks or countertrends. Once the countertrend turns out to be clear, we can pick our entrance point.

The objective is to go into a position where the countertrend will rapidly invert, and costs will swing. This is actually what empowered Jesse Livermore to procure the vast majority of his fortune.

Presently...

Before jumping into a portion of the key decides that make a swing trading procedure work, allows first look at the upsides of utilizing a basic swing trading system. You can likewise find out about planning in the swing for better trading.

The Advantages of a Simple Swing Trading Strategy?

The favorable fundamental position of swing trading is that it offers extraordinary hazard to reward trading openings. At the end of the day, you're going to change a little measure of your record balance for a conceivably a lot greater benefit, contrasted with your hazard.

The second advantage of utilizing swing trading systems that work is that it will kill a great deal of the intraday commotion. You're currently going to trade like the brilliant cash do, which is in the huge swing waves.

The third advantage of swing trading depends on the utilization of specialized markers. Utilizing specialized markers can help decrease the dangers of theoretical trading and help you to clarify choices. While some swing traders focus on major markers too, they are not required for our straightforward techniques.

The last advantage of utilizing a basic swing trading system is that you'll not be stuck to the screen for the entire day like is the situation with any day trading methodology. A swing trading plan will work in all business sectors beginning from stocks, products, Swing monetary forms, and significantly more.

Like any trading methodology, swing trading additionally has a couple of dangers. Since swing trading techniques take a few days or even a long time to play out, you face the dangers of "holes" in trading medium-term or throughout the end of the week.

Another danger of swing trading is that unexpected inversions can make losing positions. Since you are not trading all for the duration of the day, it very well may be anything but difficult to be found napping if value patterns don't happen as arranged. To diminish the danger of this event, we prescribe issuing stop orders with each new position. Stop requests can enable you "to secure" your additions and can likewise enable you to cut your misfortunes.

The ONLY pointer you truly need:

Bollinger Bands Indicator: This is a specialized pointer created by John Bollinger structured not exclusively to spot overbought and oversold domain in the business sectors; however, it likewise measures the market instability.

Our swing trading pointer makes it simple to deal with the dangers of trading, and furthermore utilize value changes. Utilizing a candle trading graph can likewise be useful. These outlines give more data than a basic value diagram and furthermore make it simpler to decide whether a supported inversion will happen.

Many swing traders additionally keep a nearby watch out for multi-day graph designs.

- Head Shoulders Patterns

- Flag Patterns

- Cup and Handle Patterns

- Moving Average Crossovers (likewise, consider the Ichimoku Cloud)

- Triangle Trading Patterns

When there are higher depressed spots alongside stable high focuses, this proposes to traders that it is experiencing a time of union. Union typically happens before a noteworthy value swing (which for this situation, would be negative). Finding out about triangle trading and other geometric trading procedures will make you a vastly improved swing trader.

This swing trading pointer is made out of 3 moving midpoints:

137

- The focal moving normal, which is a basic moving normal.

- And then on the two sides of these basic moving midpoints are plotted two other moving midpoints at a separation of 2 standard deviations from the focal moving normal.

Swing Trading Strategy that Works

This system is extremely just contained two components. The main component of any swing system that works is a section channel. For our entrance channel, we're going to utilize one of our preferred swing trading pointers, otherwise known as the Bollinger Bands. The subsequent component is a value activity-based strategy.

Step #1: Wait at the cost to contact the Upper Bollinger Band

The main component we need to see for our basic trading procedure is that we have to see stock cost moving into the overbought region. Any swing trading methodology that works ought to have this component consolidated.

Note* The favored time period for this basic swing trading technique is the 4h time span. However, the methodology can be utilized on the day by day and week after week time span too.

Step #2: Wait at the cost to Break underneath the Middle Bollinger Bands

After we have contacted the upper Bollinger Band, we need to see affirmation that we, without a doubt are in the overbought region, and the market is going to turn around. The coherent channel, for this situation, is to care for a break underneath the center Bollinger Band.

We at Trading Strategy Guides don't trade breakouts without scattering whether there are genuine purchasers/merchants – for our situation, vendors – behind the breakout which brings to the subsequent stage of our straightforward swing trading methodology.

Step #3: Swing Trading Indicator

The Breakout Candle needs to enormous a Big Bold Candle that closes close to the Low Range of the Candlestick → Sell at the Close of the Breakout Candle

So far, our preferred swing trading pointer has accurately anticipated this auction. However, we're going to utilize an extremely straightforward candle-based technique for our entrance trigger. In such a manner, we need to see a major intense bearish flame that breaks beneath the center Bollinger Band.

The second component of this candle-based technique is that we need the breakout flame to close to the low scope of the candle. This is characteristic of solid dealers, which truly need to drive this money pair much lower.

Each swing technique that works needs very basic section channels.

Presently, despite everything we have to characterize where to put our defensive stop misfortune and where to take benefits, which carries us to the subsequent stage of our basic swing trading technique.

Step #4: With we shroud our Protective Stop Loss over the Breakout Candle

The breakout flame has a great deal of significance since we've utilized it in our candle-based section strategy. We expected that this flame demonstrates the nearness of genuine vendors in the market. If the high of this light were to be broken, it's unmistakable enough this is essentially a phony breakout as there are no genuine merchants.

It's nothing muddled about it, isn't that so?

If you need to become familiar with this breakout procedure and how to oversee breakout trades, it would be ideal if you perused our Breakout Trading Strategy Used by Professional Traders article for more bits of knowledge.

The following piece of our straightforward swing trading methodology is the leave technique which depends on our preferred swing trading pointer.

Step #5: Take Profit once we crush and close spirit over the center Bollinger Bands

In this specific case, we're taking a gander at a short trading model. Thus, if the value crushes spirit over the center Bollinger Banks, it's a great opportunity to get stressed and accept our benefits as it can flag an inversion.

The motivation behind why we get the benefit here is very here to comprehend as we need to book the benefits at the early sign the market is set over.

STRATEGIES FOR BEGINNERS AND ADVANCED

With a swing trade, you are attempting to make an arrival on your venture from sensibly transient high and low moves. To do as such, you have to concentrate such market moves and discover designs that you can abuse. Take a gander at the same number of cash combines as you can, for instance, unstable moves over your preferred time period. Attempt and identify shared traits to the moves. What sort of conditions are set up when these moves happen?

Additionally, take a gander at how the value moves end. Consider the ideal method to escape a trade in such conditions. Keep in mind that swing trading is a style of trading and not a system in itself. A wide range of pointers might be fitting for this style of trading, especially any successful pattern following technique.

How about we take a gander at a model, to perceive what value swings can happen, and what dangers we may confront. You should take a gander at a lot of graphs so as to set up which technique you at long last take. The marker itself isn't especially significant for the reasons for our model. We are increasingly keen on investigating the time periods included.

In this way, we are going to utilize the accompanying pattern following system. As it comes to swing trading in MT4, you can get to an assortment of pattern following markers with the MetaTrader 4 Supreme Edition plugin, close by other ground-breaking investigation instruments.

The technique utilized here for identifying which market move to pursue isn't at all muddled. It utilizes two moving midpoints (MAs), one short, and one longer. A MA is a constantly determined number-crunching mean of the market cost for a specific number of periods. We are going to utilize a transient MA traverse a more drawn out MA. As a sign, we may see a value swing toward the cross. Alongside this pointer as our entrance signal, we will utilize the fundamental position of stops and breaking points as our methods for the exit.

The speckled red line speaks to the moving normal in the course of the most recent 25 hours. The dabbed green line speaks to the moving normal in the course of the most recent 100 hours. When the spotted red line crosses the green line, it recommends that we may see a value swing toward the cross. When does this occur?

The spotted red line (shorter MA) crosses over the dabbed green line (longer MA) occurred on 17 June at about 04:00am. We would purchase here, seeking after the upswing in the cost to proceed. Note that the upswing has just started before we get our sign. This is the manner in which moving midpoints work - they are slacking markers.

143

In our model: we would go long on the GBP/USD cash pair at 1.4280. We would then place a stop-misfortune 200 pips away, with a point of confinement of 600 pips away. We would then trail the stop 200 pips with the swing. As should be obvious from the outline, the upswing did, in fact, proceed. Our farthest point at 1.4880 would have been filled on 23 June. This was around 13:00, when the cost went as high as 1.4959 and would, in the long run, top out somewhat above 1.5000, as we moved into 24 June.

We made 600 pips, which is a solid benefit for a trade that kept going simply under seven days. The model is somewhat blameworthy of 'bend fitting.' For that are unconscious of the idea, bend fitting alludes to the example whereby a trading framework is changed and changed to intently pursue authentic data (for example, trading signals), yet it is done as such much that it results in the trading framework getting to be inadequate to use later on.

To get a legitimate thought of the viability of the technique utilized in the model, you would require to backtest it against a large number of diagrams. Presently, what might have occurred if the point of confinement was further away? Or then again if we had endeavored to pursue the upswing further by not utilizing any farthest point?

We should dependably be careful about the potential for value stuns. This is the reason you ought to dependably embrace good money the executives. Our model really gives us an impeccably genuine case of a value stun. If we expand the outline forward a bit, you will perceive any reason why.

Had regardless we had our position:

- We would have been gotten long and wrong

- The speed of the decrease would have implied that our stop-misfortune would have been confined to constrained use.

There was a drop of a few hundred pips in less than a moment. If you are found trading the incorrect path round in such a condition, it has utilized great cash the executives already. If your position is estimated effectively versus your hazard capital, it enables you to endure the hardship.

The time period of Traders

Swing is a colossally various market, and there is a wide range of approaches to pressing a benefit from it. Close by the enormous assortment of accessible trading techniques; there are likewise different trading styles. You are best off attempting to coordinate your style of trading to your very own individual needs and inclinations. One of the primary varieties in trading style is the time allotment where you work.

Long haul position players sit on the longest end of the range. These are regular traders expecting to pursue broadened patterns (which can a months ago or even a long time now and again). One of the key points of interest of long-haul trading is that it offers the potential for huge benefits, be that as it may, similar to every other type of trading, there is potential for misfortunes as well. Effectively following a pattern for a while will ordinarily exceed what can be accomplished for the time being.

Be that as it may, there's additional. Long haul trading frameworks will regularly not require much consideration past a limited quantity of checking every day. Yet, they do require a great deal of tolerance, and will probably just offer rare chances to trade. On the briefest end of the range are hawkers. Hawkers place ultra-short trades and are scanning for little value developments before leaving.

They are simply attempting to pick up a pip here and there. There is a preferred position to the incredibly short length of these trades. To be specific, you diminish your introduction to the market. It shows signs of improvement as well, since you are searching for little value developments, and open doors for trading are plentiful.

Be that as it may, the drawbacks of this include:

- A gigantic responsibility concerning time and consideration

- The necessity for incredibly well-run and taught leave the executives

- Transaction expenses can be significant in light of the high number of trades

Informal investors work a time allotment that isn't secured by hawkers and long-haul position players. These are still exceptionally momentary traders who may just hold a situation for a bunch of hours. An informal investor may utilize an assortment of strategies, however, won't hold a situation past the day's end. This implies they keep away from presentation to any market-moving stories that break medium-term.

In the middle of day trading and long-haul pattern following sits the universe of swing trading. Numerous individuals observe swing trading to be a characteristic fit since it offers an adequate trade-off between the recurrence of trades and the related time requests.

If you're simply beginning with Swing trading, or if you're searching for new thoughts, our FREE trading online courses are the best spot to gain from expert trading specialists. Get well-ordered aides on the most proficient method to utilize the best systems and pointers, and get the master sentiment on the most recent advancements in the live markets

Basic Swing Trade Strategy Explained

Swing trading is a style, not a methodology. The time period characterizes this style, and inside that, there are endless systems we can use to swing trade. Swing trading is a style that works over short to medium time allotments.

It lies between the brief span edges of day trading and the more extended time allotments of position trading.

It's not all that short that it submits all your opportunity to observe the market, yet it is short enough to give a lot of trading openings. These techniques are not select to swing trading, and just like the case with most specialized systems, backing and opposition are the key ideas driving them.

These ideas give both of you decisions inside your swing trading system including, following the pattern, or trading counter to the pattern. Counter-inclining procedures plan to benefit when backing and obstruction levels hold up. Pattern following procedures searches for the occasions when backing and opposition levels separate.

For either type, it's helpful to be able to outwardly perceive value activity. A brisk word on value activity: markets don't will in general move in a straight line. Notwithstanding when at last inclining, they go here and there in step-like moves. We perceive an upturn by the market, setting higher highs and a downtrend by identifying lower lows. Many swing trading systems include attempting to get and pursue a short pattern.

For the most part, we are seeing higher highs being accomplished, and the lows are additionally commonly rising. Even though the general pattern is up, there is a stretch in the center (from at an early stage 12 July through to 10.00 on 13 July), where there is a pullback or inversion.

During this period, the market isn't setting new highs, while the lows are moving lower and lower.

After this countertrend period, the upward pattern resumes. So, with this eyeball technique, we are expecting to discover the bullish swing, however just when we are certain enough that it will proceed. To what extent will a pullback persevere? We have no real way to know. Rather we search for affirmation that the market has returned back to its unique pattern.

As it were, we:

- Look for a pattern
- Wait for a countertrend
- Enter the market after we see the counter pattern has played out

The obvious sign that we are looking for is a resumption in the market, setting higher lows. This recommends the pullback is finished, so we would purchase the EUR/USD money pair around 16.00 on 13 July. Now we've seen the market setting progressively higher highs: and similarly, as critically, we've seen the lows of every period additionally rise.

Suppose we purchase in at 1.1082. Our first form of this system puts a stop-misfortune at the absolute bottom of the past countertrend. This level was struck at 10.00 on 11 July and was 1.1042. So our stop goes at 1.1042, and we are gambling 40 pips. The procedure is basic and goes for a hazard remunerate proportion of 1:2.

We are gambling 40 pips, so we place a point of confinement of 80 pips higher at 1.1162. This cost is come to somewhere in the range of 14.00 and 15.00 on 14 July, when the market hits a high of 1.1164. Your breaking point is then filled, and you make a benefit of 80 pips. The second form of this methodology would attempt to run the benefits much further.

In the subsequent methodology, we don't set a cutoff. For what reason don't we utilize the farthest point? Since we need to run our benefits for whatever length of time that we can. We don't have the foggiest idea to what extent the pattern may continue, and we don't have a clue how high the market can go. So, we won't attempt to make an expectation by setting a value target, yet we do realize that costs don't go straight up.

This implies you need to enable the market to move unfavorably somewhat, to appropriately ride the pattern. This additionally implies when the pattern separates, you will have given back a portion of your unrealized benefits before you close out. As opposed to utilizing a breaking point, we will put a stop at the low of the last 20 timeframes.

We never move this stop further away: however, if the 20-hour low is higher than our last stop, we would raise our stop to the 20-hour low. Extensively, this implies our stop is trailing the pattern.

The 20-hour low that characterized our stop would now have been 1.1097. We purchased in at 1.1082 and were halted out at 1.1097. We make a benefit of 15 pips. This is short of what we made with the primary system, yet meaning to run your benefits along these lines can prompt a return of high benefits when a pattern continues. These events will, in general, be rare.

Need to know the uplifting news?

Over the long haul: with the correct hazard, the executives, the benefits ought to exceed the misfortunes brought about from those occasions when the pattern separates.

Utilizing a Swing Counter-inclining Swing Trading Strategy

Our third swing trading procedure is, to a greater degree a contending trade, and in this way does something contrary to the initial two. We utilize similar standards as far as attempting to spot generally transient patterns from structure: however, at this point attempt to benefit from the recurrence with which these patterns will in general separate.

Keep in mind that as noted before:

- Increasing highs propose an upturn

- Decreasing lows propose a downtrend

We likewise perceive how an early piece of a pattern can be trailed by a time of retracement before the pattern resumes. A counter-pattern trader would attempt to get the swing in this time of inversion. To do as such, we would attempt to perceive the upswing design. Then when a new high was trailed by an arrangement of disappointments to break new highs - we go short fully expecting such an inversion.

When counter-inclining, it is critical to keep up solid order if the value moves against you. If the market continues its pattern against you, you should be prepared to concede you are incorrect and draw a line under the trade. Every one of the techniques talked about so far are exceptionally basic. They check upon the capacity to perceive and comprehend value activity.

What would traders be able to do to improve their systems? Indeed, there are a few things you can attempt. The first is to attempt to coordinate the trade with the long-haul pattern. Despite the fact that in the models above we were taking a gander at an hourly outline, it can help to likewise take a gander at a more drawn out term diagram - to figure out the long-haul pattern. Attempt and trade just when your course coordinates what you see as the long-haul pattern.

Another approach to improve your procedure is to utilize a specialized auxiliary marker to affirm your reasoning. For instance: if you are a counter-trend, and are considering selling, check the RSI (Relative Strength Index) and check whether it flags the market as overbought.

A moving normal (MA) is another marker you could use to help. A MA smooths out costs to give a more clear perspective on the pattern. Furthermore, in light of the fact that an MA fuses more established value information, it's a simple method to contrast how the present costs contrast and more seasoned costs.

Utilizing an Additional MA Indicator

This is overlaid on the EUR/USD graph that we took a gander at before. We can see that the snappier red MA line is over, the slower green MA line when we took our long position in the initial two procedures. A shorter MA being over a more extended MA is generally observed as an affirmation of an upswing. An MA is only one of the numerous amazing however easy to-utilize markers, accessible with the MetaTrader 4 Supreme Edition module.

Swing Trading Strategies - A Summary

Swing trading is a style fit for unstable markets, and it offers incessant trading opportunities. While you should put a decent lot of time into checking the market with swing trading, the necessities are not as troublesome as trading styles with shorter time spans. Once more, swing trading isn't directly for all traders - so it's ideal for rehearsing with it chance free first, on a demo trading account.

We've likewise taken a gander at some passage and leave methodologies for swing trading. In any case, it's imperative to take note of that a total swing trading framework will likewise consolidate great cash the executives, and will most likely identify reasonable markets.

Some other great practices are to:

- Avoid trading against the general pattern of the market

- Use an optional pointer to affirm a sign from your essential marker

- Have a reasonable thought of your leave edge and keep it lower than the benefit you are focusing on

- Try out your techniques in a hazard-free condition through a Swing demo account

Along these lines, if you are not trading genius, there's expectation yet. Swing trading for amateurs has numerous particular focal points, so if you are a juvenile in the financial exchanges; you can even now watch your trading benefits sore utilizing this fascinating procedure for trading. There are numerous undeniable and concealed points of interest in swing trading procedures. How about we waver from one to the next to uncover why swing trading for fledglings has the correct parity in the securities exchange.

1. Swing Trading Strategies Can Be Part-Time Too

Swing trading for fledglings does not need to be an all-day work as any individual with enough ability, and capital can swing it in the business sectors. Because of the more drawn out time allotment for swing trading for fledglings, trades can be done without steady observing and guideline. Regardless of whether you are not a full-time trader, yet a beginner, this has numerous points of interest for the individuals who can't extra time to go head-on in the business sectors.

2. Swing Trading Strategies Yields Golden Profits

If there is a silver coating in the cloud, for swing trading for tenderfoots, it is the brilliant open doors for benefits. Trade stays open for a considerable length of time or weeks, meaning traders can take advantage of higher benefits and duplicate similar security commonly in multi-day.

3. Normal Monitoring Not Required All the Time

Swing trading techniques additionally score high on other criteria, for example, setting stop misfortunes set up. Day trading means you must watch trading positions constantly. With swing trading for amateurs, the main hazard is a quit being executed at the off-base cost.

4. Swing Trading Strategies = Less Stress

Swing trading procedures are anything but a full-time occupation. Indeed, you can make benefits without investing a ton of energy in the business sectors. This implies burnout and stress will be less if you are a swing trader. You can even have normal employment or different wellsprings of salary to fix the effect of trading misfortunes in what can be portrayed as a success win situation.

5. Swing Trading Strategies Are Simple; Day Trading is Complex

Swing trading for novices can be completed with customary trading devices and a solitary PC. This does not require costly innovation or rock-solid gear, not at all like day trading.

6. Swing Trading Strategies is Popular

This is a standout amongst the most widely recognized styles utilized by traders. A significant number of the swing traders even close out positions in the wake of exploiting commercial center force. This implies clutching a situation until it pays to give up is the essential premise of swing trading for novices... something which chance disinclined traders will prize. While the commercial center can be fulfilling, it is additionally the greatest hazard for traders. Perusing patterns inaccurately can prompt sad closures to your epic trading sessions. Along these lines, swing trading methodologies have the upside of being anything but difficult to screen and beneficial for the individuals who are trying to benefit from the business sectors. Pursuing the business sectors won't go anyplace, however evaluating patterns effectively will be ideal for the individuals who need to be on the imprint constantly.

7. There's a Strategy to Swing Trading for Beginners

While traders have winning and losing trades, what is in every case increasingly significant is that additions ought to exceed misfortunes and traders ought not to lose beyond what they can bear to. Solace with trading style makes it simpler to verify benefits. Propelled traders can utilize the two kinds in their scope of trading styles. Be that as it may, amateurs would do well to ace swing trading first in view of the obvious system it includes.

8. Normal Flow Of Trading Followed

Swing trading methodologies enable novices in the market to make benefits on the normal development of the business sectors. Remember that business sectors can't move one way until the end of time. There must be some energy and snapshots of quiet in the business sectors. One can expand returns when the market ascends over and remain back when it pulls in reverse. This is the reason swing trading for tenderfoots offers continued points of interest regardless of whether you are not a pro in the business sectors.

9. Market implies Opportunity for Swing Traders

Being in and out of the business sectors, a larger number of changes can be identified than staying at one point and watching out. It is likewise simpler to diagram changes in the long haul and catch the pattern thusly. Shutting the primary position implies cash won't need to be kept to cover the subsequent one. Stop misfortunes enable you to go out on a limb without missing out on the reward.

10. Clear Boundaries Make Swing Trading Strategies Easy

Perfectly clear limits guarantee that you can break securities exchange records if you decide on swing trading. In the event that you feel that trade helps not work in out, harm control is conceivable. Long haul trading means giving a more extensive compartment to the business sectors while swing trading for amateurs offers the verifiable favorable position of a stop misfortune.

11. Major or Technical Analysis?

Swing trading systems mix specialized and major investigation to catch showcase energy and give alternatives when there is a respite. There is a productive utilization of capital just as higher returns and disadvantages include higher commission and more prominent unpredictability. Normal retail traders would not have a bit of leeway in swing trading for learners. Even though they have a more noteworthy experience, more influence, fewer commissions, and point by point data, there are restrictions in the instruments of trading they use.

Ventures in Swing Trading Strategies

For fledgling traders, swing trading procedures is significant expertise to secure. Here are the means you have to pursue to get the benefits you need to make.

1. The Opening Bell: Signal for Success

Retail swing traders start their day much before the opening chime. Truth be told, the time directly before opening is basic for getting a general feel for the market and making trades just as investigating current positions.

2. News and Views

Another assignment of the day is to make up for lost time with the most recent news and data in the business sectors. Market improvements must be checked ceaselessly for more noteworthy increases. You have to watch out for market and area feelings just as present possessions. A portion of the angles which should be observed incorporate watching out for bullish and bearish patterns, key monetary reports, swelling, cash, global trading sessions, and then some. News, money related reports, and profit are the hotly debated issues for the afternoon. Utilizing locales, for example, financial exchange filings for data will likewise assist traders with turning on the warmth in the business sectors.

3. Segment Plays: Analyzing Financial Health

Dissecting the news related with surely understood budgetary data destinations can make a comprehension of which divisions are performing admirably. For instance, the vitality area is maturing, and the higher the hazard, the more the arrival. Riding patterns to the completing post can be the mystery of accomplishment in the race for market benefits.

4. Following or Reversal? Know the Flip-Sides to Both

Diagram breaks offer a gigantic opportunity to make benefits for swing traders. These are swing trading stocks which are intensely traded close to the point of help or obstruction. From Wolfe Waves to Fibonacci levels, there are numerous approaches to anticipate how to represent the deciding moment the business sectors. A watch rundown of the swing trading stocks can likewise be made for multi-day. Swing trading stocks that look hot should make it to the rundown of related changes, the section just as target costs and stop misfortune costs.

5. Mind Existing Positions

To realize where to head in the business sectors, you should be clear about where you have been. An intensive comprehension of existing positions is an absolute necessity. Stock images can be looked into a new administration to check whether filings have been made and how this can influence trading plans and openings.

6. Watch the Markets Carefully

Markets are open at specific hours. This is an ideal opportunity to be on the watch, particularly if you are swing trading. Head phony offers and requests that set confound retail trading can be a genuine issue. The market creator should be checked while making the trade. If your moves are not couple with what's going on in the business sectors, don't hope to profit. When traders have made a few increases, they then search for the left point. This must be done through specialized investigation. Changes additionally should be completed dependent on future trading. Entering and leaving trades likewise requires significant comprehension of how the business sectors move.

7. Night-time Market: When It Really Isn't Over

Night-time trading is utilized for setting trades where the spread is an excessive amount to justify. Nightfall trading is about execution assessment. Record trades for expense and execution evaluation. Execution assessment is a significant piece of trading. During the twilight, markets are still on; however, not in fact. Focusing on after-hour income can affect the degree of benefits you make.

PURSUE THESE COMMANDMENTS OF SWING TRADING STRATEGIES

If you need to have the option to profit in the business sectors, and this is your underlying time trading, swing trading techniques can have a significant effect on benefits and misfortunes. These brilliant standards of trading will manage you how to accomplish that effectively.

1. Adjust Your Trade to Overall Market Direction

The general course of the market should be estimated by S&P. When trades and patterns are being talked about, ensure essential and middle of the road trades are dealt with. The setting wherein you settle on the choice is additionally significant. If the emphasis is just on trade, for the time being, you might pass up the master plan. Benefit potential is likewise restricted, and longer-term patterns should be identified to stream with the stream, not contradict it. Everything from news declarations to expert updates and minimizations just as acquiring hits or misses ought to dependably be guided by the bigger pattern. Long haul patterns will, in general impact the market's bearing.

2. Dissect the business sectors

When the general pattern is known, the business sectors ought not to be battled against. They ought to be worked with. Go short instead of going on and join value with respect to the record inside the graph examination. When it's bearish, search for swing trading stocks going downwards and the other way around.

3. Trade in congruity with the pattern

Keeping a nearby watch on the patterns guarantees that trading isn't undermined as far as quality. The pattern might be your companion, yet would you say you are going a similar way? Utilize moving midpoints if you need to keep in contact with patterns. This does not mean you aimlessly pursue essential patterns, as even inside the bear advertise, periods are there when the halfway pattern is certain, and swing trading stocks rise. Momentary traders ought to likewise have a thought of the master plan. Comprehend if the swing trading stocks are recounting to a story and giving some solid sign in regards to future developments. When the pattern has started, trading turns out to be progressively gainful, and hazard brings down.

4. Attempt to enter towards the beginning of the trade, not when it closes

The speedier you understand a pattern has shaped, the higher you can go up the benefits of stepping stool. Prior you get the adjustment in patterns, the more viable you will be. Focusing on the general market normal is significant in light of the fact that that which comes up must likewise go down in the end. There are numerous approaches to survey if the market is inclined to inversion, for example, the Arms Index and the Put/Call Ratio. Candles, just as force markers like stochastics, can fill in as alerts.

5. Numerous pointers are superior to just one

Trading ought not to be in a specialized device or idea in disconnection. From candles to volume and moving midpoints, a similar message resounds through with respect to either the ascent or the fall of swing trading stocks. Utilize one pointer to affirm the pattern of another.

CONCLUSION

Traders ought to dependably know when they intend to enter or leave a trade before they execute. By utilizing stop misfortunes adequately, a trader can limit misfortunes as well as the occasions a trade is left unnecessarily. All in all, make your fight arrangement early, so you'll definitely realize you've won the war.

Taking a gander at the day by day schedule of the common swing trader, it is clear that the pre-advertise routine is principal to fruitful trading. This is when trading openings are found and the day is arranged. Market hours are essentially a period of entering and leaving positions, not contriving any new plans. Lastly, night-time is only an opportunity to survey the trades for the afternoon and evaluate execution. Embracing a day by day trading routine, for example, this one can enable you to improve trading and eventually beat market returns. It just takes some great assets and legitimate arranging and arrangement.

Candles and oscillators furnish traders with a speedy and simple approach to identify swing trades. While the strategies can be utilized freely, utilizing them together is regularly progressively ground-breaking. Not all inversions are gauge by disparity or these candle designs, they are only a couple of the numerous ways that an inversion may manifest. When taking any trade, make certain to oversee chance with a stop misfortune. If going short, a stop misfortune can be put over the latest swing high, or if going long, it tends to be set underneath the latest swing low.